M000018990

"Everyone knows that the day of revivals is over and consequently the work of the evangelist has been completed, but Keith Fordham and Tom Johnston in *The Worth and Work of the Evangelist for Christ's Great Commission Church* know very well that conventional wisdom is wrong again. This superb treatment shows once again that the gifts and calling of God are irrevocable. This volume demonstrates the worth as well as the office of the evangelist and points our churches to a way to experience revival."

Paige Patterson, L. R. Scarborough Chair of Fire, Southwestern Baptist Theological Seminary, Fort Worth, TX.

"Keith Fordham and Tom Johnson have written a very needed book. They have taken the evangelism tributaries of inspiration, practical application and educational research and created a river of excellent reading. In a day when personal and revival evangelism in the SBC is not as visible, this book sends a timely message and a clear call."

Dr. John Sullivan, Executive Director-Treasurer, Florida Baptist Convention.

"Keith Fordham, long-time Southern Baptist evangelist, based here in Georgia, and Tom Johnston, Professor of Evangelism at Midwestern Baptist Theological Seminary, have teamed up to produce an amazing book on the worth and work of the evangelist. This book explains that the God-called evangelist is guardian of Christ's Great Commission for His New Testament Church. It is my prayer that God will use this book to release scores of evangelists to proclaim the Gospel message across North America and around the world."

Johnny Hunt, Senior Pastor, First Baptist Church, Woodstock, GA.

"The words of Jesus to Nicodemus apply to every living soul, 'You must be born again.' The evangelist is called by God to declare to the world that salvation is through Christ, and Christ alone. You will find this book compelling as Keith Fordham and Tom Johnston call the reader to a recommitment to evangelism and the evangelist. Chapter Ten, 'The Evangelist and God's Invitation' is a must read for every pastor. I am convinced that the only way to reach the Acts 1:8 mission field is for the church to experience a God-sent, Holy Spirit-filled, church revitalizing, sinner-saving revival! I thank God for our evangelists!"

J. Robert White, Executive Director, Georgia Baptist Convention.

"In the book of Acts we read of the remarkable spread of the Christian faith through Spirit-led living witnesses. God's Plan A for reaching the world is His children telling the good news to others, and He has no Plan B! While all believers have been commissioned to share this good news, some have been set apart as evangelists. In this practical book, Keith Fordham and Tom Johnston show the role, the call, and the work of the evangelist. This book will be a great tool for those called to this noble assignment, and to churches taking advantage of their ministry."

Alvin L. Reid, Professor of Evangelism and Student Ministry, Southeastern Baptist Theological Seminary, Wake Forest, NC.

"I have known Keith Fordham since our days in college and seminary. He has always exemplified an evangelistic spirit. He unashamedly desires to see people come to faith in Christ. Therefore, I am not surprised that Tom Johnston and Keith Fordham have written a book about New Testament evangelism. *The Worth and Work of the Evangelist* is a welcomed addition to the resources available for ministers and churches to use in their evangelistic efforts."

Rick Lance, Executive Director, State Board of Missions, Alabama Baptist Convention.

"...I am excited about the new book—so desperately needed! I pray it will be published and really promoted.

"In their book, 'The Worth and Work of the Evangelist,' Keith Fordham and Tom Johnson, have wisely brought to light a smoldering issue which must be addressed by pastors and churches all across our country. With evangelism now placed on the back burner in many churches and baptisms in a disheartening and frightening downward spiral, their study is refreshingly pertinent and timely.

"Never have our churches needed God called evangelists more—but probably wanted them less!! This casual indifference toward these divinely anointed reapers is not only a flippant rejection for the help they bring to the harvest, but far more tragically, a rather brazen disregard to the Lord Who has given and appointed them as gifts to the church.

"These insightful authors not only expose the problem, but much more importantly, they offer wise, scholarly, and Biblical instructions on how to solve it. Whether their counsel and warning will be heeded remains to be seen - but they have sounded the alarm!"

Junior Hill, Junior Hill Ministries, Hartselle, AL.

"For decades the churches have needed a resource like this that weds the best of evangelistic scholarship with the best of evangelistic practice. Dr. Keith Fordham and Dr. Tom Johnston have done both. Both men know evangelism and have practiced evangelism for decades with fruit that remains. The Worth and Work of the Evangelist can guide the evangelist in conducting an effective evangelistic ministry with integrity. It will convince the pastor to make use of this New Testament office. It can ignite fires for the Great Commission among those who serve the Lord in other capacities. Read this book, purchase multiple copies, distribute them, and implement its principles far and wide. Thank you Drs. Fordham and Johnston for this urgent contribution to a critical and neglected area of evangelism!"

David Mills, Ph.D., Th.M., Assistant Professor of Evangelism, Southwestern Baptist Theological Seminary, Fort Worth, TX.

"The work and worth of an evangelist cannot be over-stated. Never has the church needed the vocational evangelist as it does today. Please read this masterful writing and encourage others to read it and pray for revival."

Bailey Smith, Bailey Smith Ministries, Atlanta, GA.

"I urge every Pastor and layperson to read the book, 'The Worth and Work of the Evangelist.' My dear friend Dr. Tom Johnston believes in and models this gifted role that God has given to His Church. This is a scholarly approach to a task that must be re-examined by serious Churchmen. This book will bless you, convict you and lead you to take to heart the words of Paul to Timothy, 'But you, be sober in all things, endure hardship, do the work of an evangelist, fulfil your ministry.' May God use this book to bring back once again the office of the Evangelist."

Don Cass, former Director of Evangelism, Southern Baptists of Texas Convention.

"*The Worth and Work of the Evangelist* is a much-needed book for the church today. The authors have given a comprehensive Biblical and historical understanding of the call and the role of the evangelist, with ample practical application throughout the book. The God-called evangelist is a gift to the church! The church today cannot fulfill her purpose and be a fully functioning, healthy body without utilizing those who have been gifted by the Holy Spirit as evangelists. The Bible is very clear that the Lord has a very special role for the evangelist in the over-all ministry of the His church. Churches and denominations which do not incorporate evangelists into the integral functions and ministries of the church can never accomplish God's intended purpose in fully proclaiming the gospel to our culture and fulfilling the Great Commission in the most effective, efficient manner!"

Richard Harris, Consultant, North American Mission Board, Alpharetta, GA.

"I believe the book hits the nail on the head and its message needs to be heeded. … We are so wrapped up in 'programs' and reorganization that we have forgotten God has the best (only) plan that will work. He has ordained the office of the Evangelist and has given each evangelist a message to the lost. For me, I am simplistic. It is all about doing it God's way and for me, 'It's still the cross!'
"God has a plan…a plan for everything; a plan for everybody. Plugging into that plan is our responsibility. The church has in some ways foregone His plan and devised a man made plan… and we are surprised that our rate of baptisms and church membership rolls are dwindling away! We can rationalize and do as political 'spin-doctors' do and justify our plan, but only God's plan will accomplish His will and purpose. This book is a blueprint for *Church* success—and at the heart of that plan is the heart of God for His Church—succinctly expressed in Ephesians 4:11-12, 'And he gave some, apostles; and some, prophets; and some, evangelists; and some, pastors and teachers; For the perfecting of the saints, for the work of the ministry, for the edifying of the body of Christ.'

"In a nutshell, we won't succeed unless we follow that plan and it is detailed from a to z in *The Worth and Work of the Evangelist*. I enthusiastically endorse and recommend this book for evangelists, for 'would-be evangelists', for pastors, and for convention leaders."

David A. Ball, M.D., Managing Editor, *The Voice of the Evangelist.*

"One of God's given spiritual gifts is an office of an evangelist that for the most part has criticized, neglected, and underemployed, contributing to evangelistic sterility in many churches. At last, the work infusing practical methodology with modern scholarship gives church leaders a valuable manual to return the office of an evangelist to its rightful place! Read the book, reflect on it, and put it to use and see God bless your church with evangelistic harvest for His glory!"

Jake Roudkovski, Associate Professor of Evangelism, New Orleans Baptist Theological Seminary, New Orleans, LA.

"I'm convinced that this book is greatly needed. What a superb job Keith and Tom have done. It is the best synopsis possible regarding the need for simultaneous revivals, and revivals in general. Pointing out the important role of the evangelist, the biblical mandate for the evangelist, and the work of the evangelist is enlightening and inspiring.

"Fordham and Johnston have combined to pen a book concerning biblical evangelism among the best I have read in my 44 years in Southern Baptist ministry. Get the book 'The Worth and Work of the Evangelist,' read it, and apply what it teaches, for it aligns with the Bible and has been proven in history. If we as Southern Baptists hope to reverse our decline, and to reach this generation, we must practice what this book posits.

"Lay people should read this book. Many of them know nothing of the calling, life, work and need for the evangelist. They do not know how to support an evangelist. They, and their pastors, often think that the evangelists live charmed lives. If they knew the truth, they would asking their pastors why they never use an evangelist in their services and why they do not support an evangelist with prayer and finances.

"Again, this book will be required in seminaries, but simply must be read and studied in the church."

J. Mike Minnix, Former Vice President for Evangelization, Georgia Baptist Convention; founder, SermonCity; Dacula, GA.

"The book 'The Worth and Work of the Evangelist" is an excellent and needed presentation of an often ignored office: that of the Evangelist. This book is great because it is Biblical, it is Practical, it is Encouraging, and it deals with important, but often neglected, subjects. It definitely appeals to Christians and Christian leaders to get involved in Evangelism, and to recognize the special calling of an Evangelist. Dr. Tom Johnston and Evangelist Keith Fordham point to the terms used in the Bible. They describe contexts and applications of the Scripture.

"They utilize the techniques of sound interpretation. ... The writing comes out of

Bible Study and years of personal experience. I recommend this book to all."
>Jim Anderson, Chancellor Pro-Tem, Midwestern Baptist College, SBC, Kansas City, MO.

"In a day in which we are losing ground in reaching those who do not know Christ, I am thankful for a reminder of the importance of and need for the evangelist. Keith Fordham and Tom Johnston do a masterful job of presenting the role and responsibilities of the New Testament church evangelist. They provide, not only the biblical foundation for the need for these God-called men, but they also opine the responsibilities that define and maintain the evangelist's integrity. This book offers an important read for both seminarians and church practitioners."
>William D. Henard, Assistant Professor of Evangelism and Church Growth, The Southern Baptist Theological Seminary, Louisville, KY.

"In these days of declining baptisms and church attendance Keith and Tom have issued a clarion call on behalf of the evangelists and made a brilliant case for revivals. The book will help the pastor understand the evangelist and how he fits into the local church. It will help the evangelist understand his calling and place in the kingdom. And, the book will help the Convention prioritize the role and ministry of the evangelist. It is a must read for anyone serious about reaching our nation for Christ."
>Joel Southerland, State Missionary, Church Evangelism Consultant, Georgia Baptist Convention.

"Trying to pastor a church without utilizing the biblical office of the evangelist is like sitting on a three legged stool with one leg missing. You will expend too much energy just trying to keep it upright. In the book *The Worth and Work of the Evangelist*, Keith Fordham and Tom Johnson have produced a must read for any pastor who wishes to have a bible-believing, soul-winning church.
"They have built the case for the evangelist from the concept – the biblical basis and the need – to the concrete – the nuts and bolts of how to do the work. In between they have drawn a sharp contrast in the effectiveness of churches who use evangelists and those who do not. Statistics have held firm for over a decade that it takes twice as many Christians to win one person to Christ in churches that do not have revivals.
"This book should be read, re-read and put into practice by every Denominational worker, State worker, Associational worker and Administer or Faculty of our schools and seminaries. It should be required reading for every student. We must rediscover and emphasize the office of evangelist or watch our baptisms (and our churches) continue to decline."
>Petersen, Sid Peterson Evangelistic Association, Bakersfield, CA.

"Without reservation it is my pleasure to recommend this new classic on evangelism. It is burning with challenge to our Baptist Churches to bring us home to what made our Convention the most effective and fruitful Baptist Convention in the history of the

Church. This book is a must read for every Pastor, seminary student and all levels of leadership in the local church."

James I. Stewart, President, Immanuel Baptist Seminary, Sharpsburg, GA.

"An increasing number of voices have expressed doubts concerning the viability of the evangelist's role in the contemporary era. Thankfully, Drs. Keith Fordham and Tom Johnston still choose to believe. In *The Worth and Work of the Evangelist*, long-time evangelist Keith Fordham and Midwestern Baptist Theological Seminary evangelism professor Tom Johnston clearly and convincingly present the necessity of the work and role of the evangelist today. The reader will glean a greater understanding of both biblical and historical precedents concerning evangelists, as well as a greater appreciation for God-called and spiritually gifted evangelists. If you are discerning whether or not God has called and gifted you as an evangelist, or have a keen interest in evangelism, you'll not want to miss this important treatment on the subject."

Matt Queen, Assistant Professor of Evangelism, Southwestern Baptist Theological Seminary, Fort Worth, TX.

"Keith Fordham and Tom Johnston have done an outstanding piece of work in combining their scholarly research and experiences, resulting in 'The Work and Worth of the Evangelist.' Especially in a time when 'revivals' and 'crusades' have been declared by some in our convention as 'no longer effective,' this wholesome, informative and instructive book gives a clear-cut reminder that the Evangelist is a gift to the Church, the body of Christ. Well-grounded principles of evangelism coupled by revealing graphs and personal experiences, make this book not only refreshingly interesting, academically attractive, but above all, 100% Biblically sound. It will help Renew the Vision; Rekindle the Passion; and Embrace the Mandate to all readers, from the pulpit to the pew!! It is my personal pleasure to endorse this book with great enthusiasm."

John Bos, Executive Director, Christ for the World, Inc., Orlando, FL.

Eccl 10:10, "If the axe is dull and he does not sharpen *its* edge, then he must exert more strength. Wisdom has the advantage of giving success."
"The drift is to move away from evangelism. Johnston skillfully seeks to sharpen our evangelistic stroke. This work unpacks the four types of biblical evangelists, target group evangelists, practical aspects of the life of the evangelist and the breadth and scope of the word 'evangelize'. Pastoral staffs, church planter teams, teachers/small group leaders and members of the body of Christ will walk away enlightened and challenged to cease drifting away from evangelism. The Bride of Christ globally needs the evangelist to help her stay focused. I highly encourage you to read and pray through this work."

Eddy Pearson, Church Ministries/Discipleship Facilitator, Arizona Southern Baptist Convention, Scottsdale, AZ.

"It is with joy that I give my endorsement to this new book by Dr. Tom Johnston and my longtime friend Dr. Keith Fordham. The Worth and Work of the Evangelist is much needed for the day in which we live. The ministry of God called evangelists is needed as never before and this work lays that need out historically, practically, and most of all biblically. These two servants of Christ practice what they preach and are committed soul winners and preachers of the Gospel and have done a thorough job with this work. My prayer is that God would use it mightily across our Convention to stir the hearts of pastors and churches to use the ministries of vocational evangelists to the end that multitudes will hear the Good News and come to Christ."

Gary Bowlin, Former President of the Conference of Southern Baptist Evangelists; Gary Bowlin Evangelistic Association, Summit, MS.

"Every pastor, deacon and lay person should read 'The Worth and Work of the Evangelist.' It Reveals God's greatest and very neglected gift to the Church, the evangelist."

Fred McCoy, Senior Pastor, Houston Lake Baptist Church, Perry, GA.

"Evangelist Keith Fordham and Dr. Tom Johnston have given us a clear, concise, and biblical book that broaches a much needed discussion in the church. 'The Worth and Work of the Evangelist' challenges us all to take a fresh look at the office of the New Testament Evangelist. The scriptural foundation and practical application of this book will help anyone who applies them."

Bill Britt, President, Compel Outreach International, Wylie, TX.

"*The Worth and Work of the Evangelist for Christ's Great Commission Church* is an excellent resource that addresses both the spiritual and the practical aspects of the evangelist. Recent research by the Georgia Baptist Convention revealed that the churches that held at least one revival meeting per year baptized 27% more than those that did not. Churches that use a vocational evangelist and go through some type of revival preparation usually see the best results of all. Keith Fordham and Tom Johnston's book helps Great Commission churches better appreciate the role that the vocational evangelist is meant to play in their overall evangelism strategy."

Marcus Merritt, State Missionary, Evangelism Ministries, Georgia Baptist Convention.

"'In the history of the church, Evangelists are God's entrepreneurs given to the church' (p.72). In an age of excessive 'relevance' and teaching that tickles the ears, the Evangelist's entrepreneurial spirit must be sought again. Would we allow him to start something new? Would we allow him to teach us to revive a sold-out reliance on the gospel itself? This should be our desire and should manifest itself as our assistance to him in his calling to us and to the lost."

Jesse Gilliam, Pastor, Lawson Baptist Church, Lawson, MO.

"The 21st Century church needs Holy Ghost revival. God has gifted vocational evangelists in the necessary ministry of revival, renewal, and spiritual awakening. Keith Fordham and Tom Johnson have reminded us all that the office of the evangelist is still vital in this ever changing church culture. Praise God for this timely book!"

Rick Coram, Rick Coram Ministries, Jacksonville, FL.

THE WORTH AND WORK OF THE EVANGELIST

"After working 17 years on Capitol Hill at the highest level of government, I walked away in 2007 'by faith' to do the work of an evangelist. Keith Fordham was one of the first men that I met at COSBE and he inspired me then and continues to bless me today. Keith has dedicated his life to the souls of mankind and God's glorious Gospel. He is an exhorter, encourager, evangelist and expert on all things evangelism. He is not only a dean to younger evangelists but a soldier still on the streets fighting on the front lines snatching souls from Hell. In his new book 'The Worth and Work of the Evangelist' they describe in pinpoint accuracy the role that God designed for us to play in the Body of Christ. Too many view the evangelist as a threat and not a treat but the fact is we are not competition but colleagues as clergy. May this book light a fire in all whom read it that already exists in every evangelist to work together to build God's Kingdom. Together we can do so much. Individually we do so little. It is my honor to recommend this book to you and may revival start with me."

Frank Shelton, Author, FOX NEWS contributor, Evangelism Chairman, 2012 Olympics Outreach in London; Waldorf, MD.

"An invaluable resource to the beginning vocational evangelist and to pastors who hunger and thirst to see more souls saved in their church, community, county and country. In a time when among many the office of the vocational evangelist is all but ignored and revival/evangelistic meetings are counted antiquated, *The Worth and Work of the Evangelist* is must reading from the pulpit to the pew and the professor's lectern to the student's desk."

Frank Shivers, Frank Shivers Evangelistic Association, Columbia, SC.

"The book is a fresh look at the ministry of evangelism and of the evangelist. It is a must read for today's pastor."

Dennis Watson, Pastor, Harps Crossing Baptist Church, Fayetteville, GA (Keith's Pastor).

"This book is an 'imperative read' for any person who wants to really know the worth and work of a truly God called evangelist. Only a person, who has studied the factual history of the evangelist and actually experienced many years of being on the road as an evangelist, could have written such a book. That makes Tom and Keith uniquely qualified. This book is not only for the young evangelist who wants to know 'how to do it,' but for the pastor, or any person for that matter, who wants to know the physical and spiritual make up of a God made evangelist. You will find this book easy to read, and both refreshing and challenging. It could have been titled, *Every Thing You Have Ever Wanted to Know About an Evangelist.*"

Charles Massegee, Charles Massegee Evangelistic Service, Nevada, TX.

"This is a book that will benefit any evangelist or any preacher thinking God may be calling him into the work. Pastors will be inspired to use evangelists in their churches for they will see how these men can complement their ministries and edify their churches."

Phil Glisson, Phil Glisson Ministries, Memphis, TN.

THE WORTH AND WORK OF THE EVANGELIST

FOR CHRIST'S GREAT COMMISSION CHURCH

Keith Fordham and Tom Johnston

Evangelism Unlimited, Inc.
[www.evangelismunlimited.org]
Liberty, Missouri
2013

ISBN: 978-0-9831526-3-7

Published by Evangelism Unlimited, Inc.
P.O. Box 1152, Liberty, Missouri 64069-1152
www.evangelismunlimited.org

For bookstore orders, or for bulk orders (100+), email:
    tom@evangelismunlimited.org;
For all other orders, email: kfea@bellsouth.net.

For speaking information:
    For Keith Fordham, email: kfea@bellsouth.com;
    For Tom Johnston, email: tom@evangelismunlimited.org.

Cover artwork by Cory Thomason (www.corythomason.com).

DEDICATIONS

Keith would like to dedicate this book to our wives, Shirley and Raschelle, as well as to J. Dennis Watson, his pastor, to the loving people of Harp's Crossing Baptist Church, to his Sunday School teacher, Steve Wright, and his class, and to all who help support his ministry.

Tom would like to dedicate this book to his wife, Raschelle, who for 27 years has lived through many life lessons in evangelism with Tom. Then this year, Raschelle encouraged and supported Tom in his writing, chapter by chapter. Thank you.

FOREWORDS

May I commend to you the work of Evangelism Professor Tom Johnston and Evangelist Keith Fordham in this new book, The Worth and Work of the Evangelist. In this new book, we find a serious exposé of what is happening in the 21st century church regarding evangelism. Perhaps, I might say it this way; we see an exposé of the dearth of evangelism. Near the very end, Brothers Johnston and Fordham make a humorous, but serious statement when they say "the church of today is largely under house arrest." Indeed, we have closed our ears to God's plea for souls. They rightly point out that the only hope for our nation or for any people is found in the Gospel proclaimed. Sadly, they outline what has happened in our churches in the past decades that have moved our fellowships away from a serious commitment to reaching people for Christ. Many good things have taken place of the best thing. They accurately point out that the drift away from evangelism is proven throughout history.

In this work, there is also an explanation of God's call to the church. There is a strong explanation of God's call of the evangelist as a biblical office. Through history, Scripture, and testimony, they do a masterful job of explaining God's call and how it might best be accomplished. Not being tied to a singular methodology, they express in very effective ways the multiple methods that churches can use in reaching people for Christ.

There is also a powerful encouragement to the modern day church and a call to action. Pragmatic steps are shared which can help any church learn better how to reach people for Christ. There are helpful instructions in how to plan revival music. There are wonderful instructions which are very usable in revival preparation.

I encourage you to read this book carefully. More than reading the book, I encourage you to take a serious personal look at your own commitment to soul winning. When is the last time you truly shared the gospel with someone? An even stronger question is, "when is the last time you led someone to Christ?" I have often pointed out that we are seeing less personal evangelism than ever in my life. Sadly, when interviewed, even pastors confess that they are less involved than ever before. May God help us! With an estimated 258 million lost persons on this continent alone and countless millions across the world, how could it be that we are doing less sharing of the gospel than ever before?

I encourage you to read this book. I get excited when anyone is encouraging people in personal evangelism. Therefore, I commend this book to you and pray that it will be a great blessing to you and your church!

Frank S. Page, PhD., President and Chief Executive Officer, SBC Executive Committee.

I was born in the early 1940s and grew up in the 1950s when two-week revivals were the norm in many churches. As a boy, teenager and young adult I heard some of the greatest evangelists in the nation, including Hyman Appleman, Jesse Hendley, Vance Havner, Eddie Martin and J. Harold Smith.

When Billy Graham had his crusade in New York City in 1957 it lasted for 16 weeks. As a teenage boy I recall watching every one of those crusade meetings over television station WBT in Charlotte, NC. I was mesmerized by the music of George Beverly Shea and the crusade choir, the messages of Dr. Graham, the vast crowds that filled Madison Square Garden night after night and the wonderful response to the invitations. It was heart thrilling beyond description.

When I became a pastor I knew that I wanted to use God-called evangelists to preach in the revivals our church scheduled. I was so grateful for the privilege of using men like E. J. Daniels, Angel Martinez, Vince Cervera, Junior Hill, James Ponder and Bailey Smith to preach the Gospel and draw the net. I discovered that God uniquely used the preaching of these evangelists to win people to Christ that I probably would never be able to reach as a pastor. I also used music evangelists like Steve Taylor and Price Harris.

In every generation there is the danger of substituting brass for gold: man-centeredness instead of God-centeredness; a theology of glory rather than a theology of the Cross; moralism instead of Christ, sentimentalism and pragmatism instead of the Gospel; marketing instead of truth; and superficial acts of kindness instead of genuine revivals and evangelistic crusades.

Years ago C.E. Matthews, who was once secretary of evangelism for the Home Mission Board (now North American Mission Board), wrote a book entitled *A Church Revival*. In the book he wrote, "There is no substitute for preaching the gospel, and there is no substitute for mass evangelism (or revivals). To abandon mass evangelism just because it is difficult is no more excusable on the part of the pastor and church than to abandon the doctrine of repentance because it is difficult to get people to repent."

The word "evangelist" is found three times in the New Testament (Acts 21:8; Eph 4:11; and 2 Tim 4:5). This should be enough to attract our attention, because in the mouth of two or three witnesses every word is established. An evangelist is simply a messenger of the Good News, the Gospel.

In Ephesians 4:11 the Apostle Paul plainly states that Christ gave this position or work as a gift to the church in carrying out its mission. Churches that do not use evangelists are leaving out a vital part of Christ's strategic design for a healthy church. They are omitting an important piece of the divine mosaic for a growing, dynamic fellowship. To neglect the evangelist is to refuse a vital part of God's plan for the Church.

One of the unique characteristics of evangelists down through the ages has been their love for the Church and their desire to see revival fires burn. The evangelist has not only been the one to call sinners to repentance, but has also been the one who has the ability to 'stir' the hearts of the believers. Through the work of evangelists churches have been renewed in spirit and service and nations have been spared and delivered from spiritual bankruptcy.

In their marvelous book, *The Worth and Work of the Evangelist for Christ's Great Commission Church*, Keith Fordham and Tom Johnston have combined their experience and knowledge to produce a volume that is purposeful and practical. Every pastor and church leader should read this valuable offering and discover anew the value of having the evangelist "stir the coals and keep the fires of the Great Commission burning in every local church."

J. Gerald Harris, Editor, *The Christian Index*.

PREFACE

I first met Tom Johnston in 1999 at the Conference of Southern Baptist Evangelists' Retreat. As we spent time together, I discovered that Tom has a genuine heart for souls, evangelists, and evangelism. Tom radiates Jesus and we instantly knew we were like minded. I loved Tom Johnston from the day we met. For the next eight years we met at the evangelists' retreats sharing our hearts.

Tom and I collaborated in teaching the course "The Work of the Evangelist." I found that Tom not only teaches evangelism, he practices it, and requires his students to do the same. As part of the course, we went out with his students to win disciples on the streets of Kansas City. In conjunction with the class, a revival was held in the church where he was interim pastor. On another occasion I preached a tent revival when he was interim pastor at Lawson, Missouri. Souls were saved every time because he taught people to witness in the power of the Holy Spirit and expected God to give the increase.

During these days we talked about rewriting my book *The Evangelist Born in the Heart of God*. The fact is that all of us need to return to the Great Commission. This includes Southern Baptists and other evangelical denominations. "Every Christian Evangelizing" is the Bible standard. "The Worth and Work of the Evangelist" came out of much prayer and studying God's Word. Our goal is to inspire the 21st Century church to utilize Christ's gift of the evangelist to carry out the Great Commission.

As President of the Conference of Southern Baptist Evangelists, I invited Tom to speak on "Toward Translating Evangelize as Evangelize!" at the evangelists' retreat. His teaching was straight from the word of God. He introduced us to the Greek word *euangelizo* (evangelize). Acts 8:4 says "So those who were scattered went on their way evangelizing the word" (Logos=Jesus). 1 Cor 9:16, "For if I evangelize, I have no reason to boast, because an obligation is placed on me. And woe to me if I do not evangelize!" His background in the biblical languages of Greek and Hebrew, and also in Latin and French (his native tongue) gives him deep insight and understanding in the word of God. Reading these other languages gives him the ability to research freely in books not written in English. This adds a depth of knowledge that makes him a "walking encyclopedia" on church history and doctrinal studies.

Tom said things "off the cuff" that made me slap myself on the forehead and say "Man, that is so obvious, I should have seen that!" For instance he pointed out that only 3% of a minister's education is evangelism. Our seminaries need to provide a Great Commission education to produce winners of souls for Christ. Half of the classes should be in the area of evangelism. Classes should be taught such as "Preaching Christ from the Old Testament." Theology should be changed to Gospelology. This Great Commission approach would permeate our students with "Every Christian Evangelizing." Not one student would graduate from seminary without leading a soul to Christ. A true Great Commission curriculum would place students in situations where they can lead people to our Kinsman Redeemer the Lord Jesus Christ.

Tom used his ability to put our words and thoughts into charts. His chart on "The Synergistic Power of Simultaneous Revivals" shows clearly the only method that unites Baptists. Simultaneous revivals lift church planting, church growth, discipleship, Sunday school, personal evangelism, every type of evangelism, Brotherhood, Women's ministry, Student Ministry, Children's ministry, missions, RA's, GA's and all other ministries of the church. When Simultaneous method is the focus even our colleges, universities, seminaries, state conventions, associations, and local churches are strengthened. If any other focal point is used it splinters and divides the denomination. Every other method tends to lose focus on other methods and ministries. Simultaneous revivals unite and lift up all other areas of ministry. Tom's chart on Baptisms in the SBC shows the historic cycle of downturn in baptisms and cooperation until we return to the simultaneous revival synergy powered by the Holy Spirit.

Thank God for cell phones and emails. This made it possible for us to stay in constant contact during the writing of this book. We shared our hearts and insights as we worked in partnership. Thank God for airplanes that made it possible for Tom to fly to Atlanta and spend three days in my home as we prayed and worked together. God's Spirit opened our eyes as we studied the scripture and slaved over this manuscript. "Iron sharpens iron" and "two are better than one," became realities as we labored together. The Bible methods of the New Testament work today just as they did 2000 years ago. People have the same need for God that only Jesus can fill. No matter what culture or time in history men need Christ, His forgiveness and resurrection power to live in this wicked world. Men will always need Christ, now and through all eternity. As long as this present earth stands, God's method will be the Great Commission people reaching others with the glorious gospel of the Lord Jesus Christ.

Tom's insight concerning how the office of Evangelist is used by Christ to protect against doctrinal error and drifting away from the Great Commission was another of those obvious facts that I had overlooked. Tom's knowledge of the recent History of evangelism along with Chuck Kelley's *How Did They Do it? The Story of Southern Baptist Evangelism* reminded me how God used this method to get me under the Word of Christ so I could be saved.

God's hand in the simultaneous revival method reached me. I grew up in a construction family. I was born in Griffin, Georgia. I took my first steps in Modoc, South Carolina. I lived in Gainesville, Starke, Flagler Beach, Mayport, and other assorted Florida cities. My baby brother was born in Wilmington, North Carolina. Knoxville, Tennessee, along with Chamblee and Mountain View, Georgia, were stops along the way. When my dad was asked to move to New Orleans, he told his boss, "No." He went into business with my Uncle Jack and we stayed in Forest Park, Georgia so I could finish High School.

Attending church with my next door neighbors put me under the hearing of the gospel message. From the pulpit to the Sunday school class to Royal Ambassadors and Christian Training and even in the singing I heard of Jesus' death, burial, resurrection and power to save. But it took the synergistic moving of God through an evangelist, a church revival, and a revived Christian, to lead me to Christ on October 30, 1960. My pastors, church family, and personal family did the follow up, along with evangelist after evangelist and revival after revival.

I answered the call to the ministry in December 1967 and preached my first sermon in January 1968. It was pathetic. I did such a poor job I told the Lord I would never preach again. God intervened and I was called to preach a youth night at First Baptist, Mountain View, Georgia. I told the Lord I would preach if He gave me a sermon. He did and heaven came down. I preached my first revival at my home church that summer and now over 1,500 revivals and harvest days later I am still going on.

Tom and I had very different upbringings. Tom was born to missionary parents in France. He was saved at the age of four on the knee of his mother, after he had done wrong at the local French school. He was baptized by his father at the age of thirteen, again in France. Although he went forward on several occasions to dedicate his life to the ministry, it was in seminary that the Lord wooed Tom's heart to the cry of dying souls. It was through a requirement in an evangelism class, for which he had to turn in ten contact reports that the lostness of people all around him began to tug at his heart. Following this class, Tom began an evangelism team at that school so that he could practice weekly evangelism. This discipline has been his practice for most of his life. He was licensed to preach in the Christian and Missionary Alliance denomination in Quebec-City, Quebec, in 1986 and was ordained at Springdale Church in Louisville, Kentucky, in 2001.

Tom earned a Ph.D. in evangelism at the Southern Baptist Theological Seminary in Louisville in 2001, and was asked to teach evangelism at Midwestern Baptist Theological Seminary by its president, R. Philip Roberts. He has been teaching evangelism at Midwestern since that time, as well as some undergrad church history and Baptist history classes. In all, Tom has served as pastor or interim pastor at seven churches and as an instructor or professor of evangelism at ten seminaries, colleges, or Bible schools. Any weakness in the writing comes from me. Thank God most of "The Worth and Work of the Evangelist" is written by Tom and will thrill your soul.

In "The Worth and Work of the Evangelist" you will discover that evangelists are catalysts sent by Christ to stir the church and stimulate the people of God to win the lost. The Lord Jesus will see to it that His church will always have evangelists. The scripture teaches that Philip the Evangelist was already doing "Every Christian Evangelizing" before he became an evangelist. The next generation of evangelists will come from churches where "Every Christian Witnessing" is practiced and where churches have evangelists in the pulpit for the people to be exposed to and influenced by the office of the evangelist. This is the Bible way.

Matt 9:38 "Therefore, pray to the Lord of the harvest to send out workers into His harvest." The words "send out" are one Greek word. Ekballo (ἐκβάλλω) means to bring forth, or cast out, or drive out. It is the same word used for Jesus driving out the money changers from the temple. During the Jesus movement of the late sixties and early seventies I was at Samford University. Any revival service we entered we would pray, "Lord, for the beating we are about to receive, we give You thanks!" We knew the evangelist was going to challenge us to get right with God and win people to Jesus. The Evangelist did and we did. Praise God!

When you finish reading this book you will pray, "Lord, make me a soul winner, and Lord Jesus, please give us more evangelists!" The next thing you will do is have a revival using a Christ-given evangelist!

Yours For Souls,
Keith Fordham, D.Min.
Fayetteville, Georgia

Like no other church leader, the name "evangelist" represents a methodology. He represents the primacy of heralding the gospel. Because he believes that "faith comes by hearing, and hearing by the word of Christ" (Rom 10:17), the evangelist wants people to hear. His methodology is one of speaking and proclaiming. It is one of initiating evangelism opportunities. Like no other leader in Christ's church, the evangelist, by his very name, represents an assertive approach. While the title "teacher" is found at every level of society associated with every form of belief, it is not so with the name "evangelist." While the title "pastor" has a spiritual connotation, it is associated with the work of a shepherd in caring for his flock, it is not so with the "evangelist." Both deacon and elder are used in a variety of churches and represent multiple means of oversight. But the name "evangelist" represents a specific methodology, that of the assertive proclamation of the gospel of Jesus Christ.

Like no other church leader, the name "evangelist" also represents a doctrinal position. The title "pastor" does not presuppose a doctrinal position. There are pastors that represent every shade of doctrine. Nor does the title "teacher" presuppose a doctrinal position. There are teachers in every world religion and for every form of science. But the title "evangelist" presupposes belief that faith comes by hearing, and hearing by the word of Christ. The title "evangelist" presupposes belief in "you must be born again" (John 3:7). By his very association with the "evangel," (Gospel) the evangelist believes that Jesus is the only way of salvation: "There is no other name under heaven given by which we must be saved" (Acts 4:12). The title "evangelist" presupposes belief in the Substitutionary Atonement and in justification by faith. All these doctrinal positions are imbedded in the title "evangelist" with very little wiggle room.

So, the title "evangelist" is like a winnowing fork. By its very nature it carries with it a host of presuppositions. God has providentially kept this title very narrowly defined. And for this reason the evangelist suffers the reproach of the gospel. Those who do not agree either with his methodology or his doctrinal position find fault with him. This is certainly why B. H. Carroll said so many years ago when speaking of evangelists, "Deny not fins to things that must swim against the tide, nor wings to things that must fly against the wind."[1] The evangelist is a divine burr under the saddle of the church and culture, keeping both in check.

Notice the wise words of R. G. Lee as to God's providential protection of his church through the ministry of the evangelist:

> "The Purpose of the Conference of Southern Baptist Evangelists has been to encourage Bible preaching, gospel singing, and personal witnessing. These are the endeavors that have strengthened Southern Baptists when other denominations have moved away from these fundamentals and weakened their position."[2]

In the history of U.S. denominations, as long as the evangelist was held in high esteem, the gospel radiated forth from those denominations. When their worth and work waned, so did the doctrinal positions of those denomination. R. G. Lee wanted to encourage this group of men and women to flourish in the Southern Baptist Convention. For as go the evangelists, so goes the denomination.

This book examines the worth and work of the evangelist. It represents a cooperative effort between me, a professor of evangelism, and Keith Fordham, a long time vocational evangelist. It is our desire that God will use this book to call forth, mobilize, and encourage multiple dozens and hundreds of evangelists to minister in Christ's harvest. Truly, the harvest is plentiful, but the laborers are few.

Thomas P. Johnston, Ph.D.
Liberty, Missouri
August 2012.

---

[1]B. H. Carroll, "Shall the Atlanta Board Be Instructed to Employ Evangelists and to Call for an Extra $25,000 for Their Support?" *Baptist Standard* (31 May 1906) 14:1-2; cited in Charles S. Kelley, Jr., *How Did They Do It? The Story of Southern Baptist Evangelism* (New Orleans: Insight, 1993), 14.

[2]R. G. Lee, "Foreword," in John Scott Trent, *Evangelists in Action: History of the Conference of Southern Baptist Evangelists.* Foreword by Robert G. Lee (Orlando, FL: Daniels, 1971), 8.

TABLE OF CONTENTS

CHAPTER ONE

THE HISTORICAL CONTEXT
FOR THE EVANGELIST

"In the course of the spread of Christianity,
God has called men into special service as evangelists."

Preamble,
Constitution of the Conference of Southern Baptist Evangelists

The discouraged Elijah complained to God after he had the amazing Mount Carmel experience of the power encounter against the 450 prophets of Baal and the 400 prophets of the Asherah, all of whom had eaten at Jezebel's table. He had personally slaughtered them down by the Brook Kishon (1 Kings 18:40)! Then he ran from the queen who sought his life. As he was hiding in a cave, God called to him two times, saying, "What are you doing here, Elijah?"

After Elijah told God of his zeal for the name of the Lord. After his repetition of the same words, the still small voice commissioned him to anoint three people. God was prophesying the inevitable downfall of King Ahab and Queen Jezebel. Yet in that same prophetic portion, God made an interesting statement, to help release Elijah from his introspective self-pity. God spoke of others in the country that had not given in to the religious norms of the wicked king and queen:

> "Yet I have reserved seven thousand in Israel, all whose knees have not bowed to Baal, and every mouth that has not kissed him" (1 Kings 19:18)

God did not say, "I have reserved seven thousand prophets who are proclaiming My name." Nor did God say, "Seven thousand men have kept themselves from bowing to Baal." God, in His sovereignty, had kept for Himself seven thousand who had not bowed their knee to Baal. They had not given in to the decadence and immorality of their time. They, in essence, were those who had heeded the words of Elijah!

In a way, this was a negative proposition from God. Seven thousand had not bowed the knee to Baal. Yet, if the people of Israel accounted for five million people in that time, then 7,000 was a very small percentage. While numbers are difficult to find for the exact population of Israel at the time, Jehoshaphat, King of Judah during the reign of Ahab in Israel, had a standing army of 1 million 160 thousand men (2 Chron 17:14-19). If we consider that Israel's army was about the same size, for the 10 northern tribes, and if we consider that the military men per total population ratio is about 1:4, then let us assume that Israel had a population of about 5 million people (*Smith's Bible Dictionary* conjectured 4,640,000 people). In that case, 7,000 who have not bowed the knee to Baal represents only 0.14% of the population. The actual percentage is likely even less than that.

So, what was God trying to tell Elijah with the figure of 7,000 men?

- You are not alone, as you keep repeating to Me!
- I am working out my perfect will; please allow Me to do so!
- Don't focus on the numbers, remain faithful!

Like Elijah, evangelists become discouraged. Going from church to church, occasionally evangelists may receive an honorarium which is not enough to pay travel expenses. That means there is no personal income for personal or ministry needs. Some pastors have not prepared and the turnout (as can be expected) is not that great. At other times it is difficult even to get someone to say, "Amen!" during the sermon, much less get people to the point of making decisions for Christ. God would tell you, dear evangelist, "Press on!" Evangelist, you need to know that you are doing God's will in God's way. This knowledge will give you strength. Remember Elijah and the 0.14% of the population who were faithful to the Lord.

Sometimes we read or hear of large churches and their growth. One only needs to compare the attendance in all the Bible-preaching churches on any given Sunday with the total population of the cities or towns from which they draw people. If this calculation is done, then one's view of the total number of faithful in any town or city will be brought down to size. God does not appear to mind when His people are in a minority, even when there is a great prophet among them, like Elijah.

In that light, it does not seem to bother God that His evangelists seem to be in a minority either. While we read of the massive crusades of a D. L. Moody, Wilbur Chapman, Billy Sunday, and Billy Graham, there were also the faithful ministries of thousands of evangelists who are sometimes forgotten, for example Mordecai Ham, Hyman Appelman, and Angel Martinez. The COSBE "Hall of Faith" highlights some of these great men at http://www.sbcevangelist.org/ Hall-of-Faith.html. There are also writings highlighting the ministries of evangelists from years gone by, for example:

- Earl Cairns, *An Endless Line of Splendor: Revivals and Their Leaders from the Great Awakening to the Present* (Tyndale House, 1986).
- Charles S. Kelley, *How Did They Do It? A History of Southern Baptist Evangelism* (Insight, 1993).
- Paulus Scharpff, *History of Evangelism: Three Hundred Years of Evangelism in Germany, Great Britain, and the United States of America* (Eerdmans, 1964).
- Also see Ed Reese's "Christian Hall of Fame" series (Glenwood, IL: Fundamental Publishers).

Not all of the thousands of evangelists that have spanned the country and the globe are forgotten. In addition, God keeps the best records, and He mightily rewards His servants according to their service.

However, there appears to be some common statements when it comes to evangelism and evangelists:

- "Today, there are fewer evangelists going into the work!"
- "It used to be better for evangelists, some 30-50 years ago!"
- "Now is a really tough time for most evangelists!"

Amazingly, we hear or read these negative statements over and over again, at different points in history. Nevertheless, God, in His infinite wisdom, allows that His primary Great Commission leader, the Evangelist, has plenty of push-back and enough friends to keep him on the right path.

- **On the Ebb and Flow of Evangelists**

Why is it, that in any and every period of church history, it appears that evangelists go through tough times? While there are ebbs and flows, the ebbs seem to be more common than to flows. Listen, for example, to words of B. H. Carroll as to hardships in the ministry of the evangelist in 1906:

> "The bedrock of Scripture underlies it. Experience demonstrates its wisdom and feasibility. If the Home Mission Board may employ any man, it may employ evangelists. Altogether, then, with a ring, let us support this measure. If I were the secretary of the board I would come before this body in humility and tears and say: 'Brethren, give me evangelists. Deny not fins to things that must swim against the tide, nor wings to things that must fly against the wind.'"[1]

It is amazing, that more than 100 years later, the same words could be spoken of evangelists today. Evangelists today "swim against the tide" and they "fly against the wind." In 1949, C. E. Matthew's hinted at the same thing, when he wrote:

> "Evangelism is the spearhead of the attack against the forces of evil in this world. It is the vanguard in the conquest of God's great army against the gates of hell as we try to rescue the deluded victims of

---

[1]B. H. Carroll, 14:1-2; cited in Charles S. Kelley, Jr., *How Did They Do It: The Story of Southern Baptist Evangelism* (New Orleans: Insight, 1993), 14.

4

Satan and lead them from darkness to light. Evangelism kindles and rekindles the flames of compassion in the hearts of all Christians and especially in the hearts of preachers, teachers, and church officers in our local churches. Without it, we drift into cold, clammy formalism and ritualism that breathe the breath of stagnation and death into church life. If we are agreed on this, then we ought to give evangelism its rightful place in our denominational life."[2]

This struggle continues to exist even today.

After the stirring words of Carroll in 1906, the SBC Convention vote for a Department of Evangelism passed, and W. W. Hamilton became the director of the department. Hamilton used the "Pittsburg Plan" of simultaneous revivals, and had a salaried group of evangelists that he called his "Stable of Evangelists."[3] The love offerings from churches went right back into the Department of Evangelism. This was the only department of the Home Mission Board that was ever self-supporting. Hamilton's strategy for revival also included training for "personal work," (or "personal evangelism"). He described his evangelists:

"It is composed of white and Negro evangelists and singers, who are paid a regular salary, and who go on mission fields, to weak and strong churches in country and town and city. They hold individual or group meetings, and as occasion offers the staff of workers is brought together for an associational or city or State campaign, conducting meetings as far as possible in every Baptist church at the same time, and having a great central service daily in which instruction in personal work is given and where music, definite prayer, reports of meetings, and inspirational preaching are features."[4]

Meanwhile, B. H. Carroll went on to found Southwestern Baptist Theological Seminary in 1908. The school soon became a beacon for revival evangelism, following in the footsteps of its founder. During that time Evangelists like J. Wilbur Chapman and R. A. Torrey were

---

[2]C. E. Matthews, *The Southern Baptist Program of Evangelism* (Atlanta: Home Mission Board of the Southern Baptist Convention, 1949), 8.

[3]Charles S. Kelley, *How Did They Do It*, 18-19.

[4]Ibid., 19.

holding city-wide crusades. Evangelists like Billy Sunday, Mordecai Ham, and many other evangelists also spoke out against the dangers of alcohol. In fact, Sunday's most famous sermon became his "Booze Sermon." These powerful thrusts of the Sword of the Lord led to the Prohibition Era in U.S. history. It was an era of increased prosperity and decreased crime for the U.S.

Then in 1927, author Sinclair Lewis published a satirical novel describing the life of a fictitious evangelist named "Elmer Gantry." Although it created public outrage and was banned in Boston, "*Elmer Gantry* ranked as the number one fiction bestseller of 1927, according to 'Publisher's Weekly'" (Wikipedia). Meanwhile, the SBC suffered the tragedy of the 1928 embezzlement by its treasurer. In the wake of this occasion, the Department of Evangelism was dissolved. It appeared that the era of revivals and mass evangelism was coming to a close. In fact, William Warren Sweet wrote in 1930:

> "Revivalism still continues in many parts of the United States, especially in the South and in rural areas throughout the country, but it is no longer the universal technique of the evangelical churches. The conditions which produced it have been gradually passing, and will doubtless continue to do so. Most of the churches which formerly depended upon the revivalistic method for winning converts are now in the throes of trying to find new methods of approach"[5]

Regardless of this malevolent prophecy of the passing of revivals, graduates from Southwestern, New Orleans, Moody, Bob Jones, Nyack, and a host of other Bible colleges and seminaries were going out as revivalists, evangelists, pastors, and missionaries. Perhaps they did not expect a warm welcome from the world, because Christ had forewarned them to expect negativity (Matt 10:16-26). So God kept raising up more and more evangelists like Porter Barrington, Cliff Brannon, Vince Cervera, E. J. Daniels, Charles Fuller, Freddy Gage, John Haggai, Randy Haman, Joe Henry Hankins, Jesse Hendley, Bob Jones, Sr., Clyde Kendall, Eddie Lieberman, Eddie

---

[5]William Warren Sweet, *The Story of Religion in America* (San Francisco: Harper and Row, 1950), 346-347.

Martin, Walter "Happy Mac" MacDonald, John R. Rice, Ed Vallowe, and Don Womack.

In 1936 the Department of Evangelism was reconstituted under the leadership of Roland Q. Leavell. In 1946, Leavell became president of the newly named "New Orleans Baptist Theological Seminary." That next year, C. E. Matthews became director of the Department of Evangelism. Matthews initiated an incredible era of evangelism throughout the SBC, sometimes called the "Golden Age" of Southern Baptist evangelism. In 1949 he authored *The Southern Baptist Program of Evangelism*. He explained, "The main fault is that there is no soul-winning program in these churches."[6] This book explained and promoted a strategy of simultaneous revivals:

> "The only method in evangelism, we believe, that is absolutely adequate for this hour is the simultaneous method. A simultaneous revival is one in which all of the churches of like faith and convictions within a given territory enter into a revival beginning on the same day and closing on the same day. No other kind of meeting is simultaneous."[7]

One excellent example of Matthews applying this focus in simultaneous revival was in his work with the Sunday School Board's J. N. Barnette. In the early 1950s, Barnette coined the phrase, "Million More in '54," as a special recruiting effort in preparation for the simultaneous revival that was being planned by C. E. Matthews.[8] Matthews gathered the cooperation of the various SBC entities, combined their efforts with various branches of the local church, all of which were cooperating in multiple types of evangelism, with mass evangelism as the strategic gathering point. His approach was "cooperative, coordinated, unified evangelism."

[6]Matthews, *The Southern Baptist Program of Evangelism*, 7.

[7]Ibid., 40.

[8]"Another push to increase Sunday school enrollment came in 1954 with the 'Million More in '54,' a program developed by J. N. Barnette intended to enroll one million more individuals in Sunday school" (John L. Rothra, "History of Personal Evangelism Training within Local Church of the Southern Baptist Convention"; available at: http://www.jrothraministries.com/pdfdocs/HistoryofEvangTraininginSBCChurches.pdf [online]; accessed 27 July 2012; Internet).

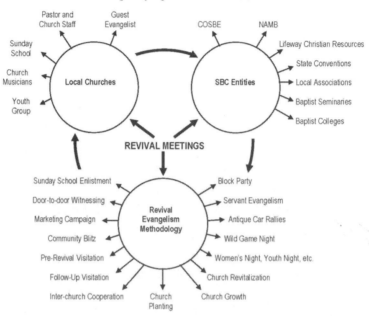

TABLE 1: Harnessing the Synergistic Power of Simultaneous Revivals

Table 1 graphic portrays this synergy of cooperation. Under the leadership of C. E. Matthews and J. N. Barnette, the SBC harnessed this synergy of the simultaneous revival in the late '40s and '50s. It was truly a time that can be described as "All at it, always at it!" And God's Word bore great fruit. The result was the golden age of growth in the SBC.

When "Revival Meetings" are at the center of the diagram, then the doctrine of the whole enterprise is protected by the ministry of the evangelist. Jesus and His cross are at the central focus. The Word of God and conversion remain primary. Consider, for example, the poignant words of R. G. Lee:

> "The Purpose of the Conference of Southern Baptist Evangelists has been to encourage Bible preaching, gospel singing, and personal witnessing. These are the endeavors that have strengthened Southern

Baptists when other denominations have moved away from these fundamentals and weakened their position."[9]

If something other than "Revival Meetings" are placed at the center of the diagram, then unintended consequences result. There is a shift away from:

- Faith comes by hearing, and hearing by the word of Christ (Rom 10:17);
- The word of God never returns void, but always accomplishes its work (Isa 55:11);

Thus…

- People coming under the hearing of the word of Christ through Sunday School ("Million More in '54") and in the preaching service,
- Equals more people prepared to respond to the invitation of the evangelist when he comes for revival meetings.

Further, when "Revival Meetings" are removed from Great Commission churches, God's protection and Christ's provision over the Great Commission through the ministry of the God-called evangelist is lost. For example, if "Church Growth" is placed at the center of the diagram, the doctrinal focus of the evangelist, as described above by R. G. Lee, is dissipated. Anyone who for whatever reason wants to grow their church, regardless of their theology, will join the movement. Further, the synergy gained by the simultaneous revival method is lost.

It must be remembered that what today are called, "Special Events," "Special Evangelistic Events," or "High Impact Events," were all developed within the context of revival meetings. Each of these developed as special evening emphasis to draw people to hear the gospel at the revival meeting. Including revivals as a subset of special events, appears to be falling prey to the fallacy of

---

[9]R. G. Lee, "Foreword," in John Scott Trent, *Evangelists in Action: History of the Conference of Southern Baptist Evangelists*. Foreword by Robert G. Lee (Orlando, FL: Daniels, 1971), 8.

composition, in other words, falsely grouping items together as if they carry the same weight.

As the South was being reached by simultaneous revivals, a new face appeared in the Northern states, the preacher from North Carolina, Billy Graham. When Billy Graham preached his famous Los Angeles Tent Meeting in 1949, he had already been preaching revivals since 1938, preaching four Youth for Christ rallies in 1944, and 20 rallies in 1946. His book, *Calling Youth to Christ*, was published in 1947, the same year he became President of Northwestern Bible College, founded by W. B. Riley, pastor of First Baptist Church, Minneapolis. After his 1949 Los Angeles crusade, Evangelist Billy Graham became a rising star in U.S. and world Evangelicalism. The titles of his next two books, *Revival in Our Time* (two 1950 editions) and *America's Hour of Decision* (1951), give an example of the expectancy generated by Graham's early ministry.

For the next 25 years, following World War II, the ministries of many Evangelists in the U.S. were in an upswing, particularly in the Southern states. It was during these years of harvest that COSBE (Conference of Southern Baptist Evangelists) was founded. However, before continuing with this storyline, perhaps it may be appropriate to discuss the evangelistic drift that took place in the Northern States from the 1960s to the present.

- **Considering Drift in Methodology of Evangelism**

Following the "golden age of revival" among Southern Baptists, there appeared to be significant decline in churches using evangelists and the revival methodology. Simultaneous revival became institutionalized, without biblical and theological conviction. And a there appeared to be a drift in methodology of evangelism. This drift appears to have been more noticeable among Northern Evangelicals in the U.S.

Table 2 explains several cyclical patterns involved in this evangelistic drift. These cyclical patterns are evident in three phases

TABLE 2: The Northern Shift from Revival Evangelism

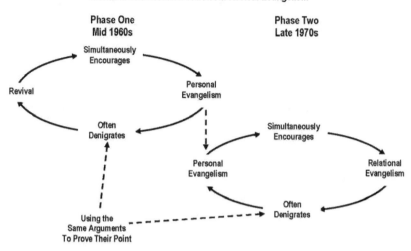

of change in methodology of evangelism, which, most importantly, have different theological bases from which they function:

1. From Revival Evangelism (1960s) to Personal Evangelism (1970s);
2. From Personal Evangelism (1970s) to Relational Evangelism (1980s);
3. From Relational Evangelism (1980s) to Servant Evangelism (1990s).

These phases are not meant to shock the reader nor to vilify certain authors or methods, but rather to portray paradigm shifts experienced by these authors, and affirmed by a study of books published in the area of evangelism. Table 2 graphically portrays this drift in two cyclical patterns.

Whereas those who promote, conduct, and preach revivals also support and promote personal evangelism training and efforts, their companions, the personal evangelists, may not do so. Revivalists ask churches to canvas neighborhoods, share the gospel, and invite their neighbors. Personal evangelists, however, often prefer hitting the streets where there are lost people. Consider the words of Matthews on this point:

"Mass evangelism does more than personal [evangelism] to bring lost sinners to Christ. Mass evangelism revives the people of God; personal evangelism puts them to work. Without mass evangelism, a congregation becomes complacent, spiritually cold, and indifferent. Worldliness takes over and the church loses its attractiveness and power. Baptisms decrease in number; factionalism develops in the church, creating divisions and strife and usually ending in the resignation of the pastor. The church quits majoring on the saving of souls and places chief emphasis on fellowship and social service, leaving the lost in the community to die in their sins."[10]

According to Matthews, revival evangelism does *more* than personal evangelism to bring people to Christ. That is quite a statement in itself! In fact, the above cycle portrays the drift in the opposite direction. The reasons given for moving away from revival evangelism are to be expected:

- Revivals don't work in our day and culture;
- Likewise, revivals are old fashioned, out-dated, and irrelevant;
- People in this generation* are more relational than they used to be, propositional evangelism no longer works for them.

    *Various titles forwarded to describe "this generation" were and are: in the 1910s-1930s: Industrial Man; 1940s: Atomic Man; 1960s: Revolutionary Man, Cosmic Man, or Existential Man; 1980s: Boomers; 1990s: Busters or Gen Ex; 2000s: Gen Y or Millennials; etc.

Each successive generation provides "scholars" in evangelism new ammunition to invalidate New Testament evangelism. The doctrinal and methodological integrity of the church, providentially provided by God through the ministry of His evangelists, is lost.

In a strange turn of the tables, the same arguments that personal evangelists sometimes use against revival evangelists eventually turn against them. So, in the North in the 1960s, when revivals were phasing out, the personal evangelism methodology of *Evangelism Explosion* (Tyndale House, 1970) was phasing in. A decade later

---

[10]Matthews, *The Southern Baptist Program of Evangelism*, 9-10.

Northern Evangelicalism was hit by a barrage of books not too friendly to aggressive personal evangelism. These included Becky Pippert's *Out of the Saltshaker* (InterVarsity, 1978), Jim Petersen's *Evangelism as a Lifestyle* (NavPress, 1980), and Joe Aldrich's *Life-Style Evangelism* (Multomah, 1981). As a result, while SBC churches were using CWT (Continuous Witness Training), their Northern counterparts began to phase out *Evangelism Explosion*, with very little to replace it.

Then toward the end of the 1980s, Jim Petersen's *Living Proof* (NavPress, 1988) was published. It sought to fill this void in local church methodology. Petersen taught that friendship or relationship was a necessary prerequisite prior to sharing the gospel. After that, Steve Sjogren authored *Conspiracy of Kindness* (Vine Books, 1993) espousing, for his part, that the best kind of evangelism necessitated some type of act of kindness as a necessary prerequisite or preparatory grace. By that time, most Northern Evangelical churches were at least 30 years from ever having a revival. Currently, many Evangelical churches in the North struggle to know how to do any type of evangelism, most New Testament forms have been rejected as culturally irrelevant. And yet, New Testament evangelism works in every situation as it always has!

Neither has the South been immune to the chilling effects of publishing efforts of their Northern counterparts. While many churches in the South continue to use revivals on a regular basis, Evangelists in states such as Missouri, have found it difficult in these past 10-15 years.

A brief word about New Testament methodology may be appropriate here. Rather than pit personal evangelism versus revival evangelism, the Bible holds them both in a balanced synergy. In fact, God foreknew that personal evangelism versus mass evangelism would be an issue of debate among His people. So, when the role of the evangelist is introduced via the ministry of Philip, the only named evangelist in the Bible (Acts 21:8), we read of both forms of evangelism. We read of him holding a city-wide revival in Acts 8:5-14. His audience is clearly a plurality:

- v. 5, "city of Samaria"
- v. 6, "the multitudes with one accord"
- v. 8, "And there was great joy in that city"
- v. 9, [of antithetic], "in the city"
- v. 9, [of antithetic], "people of Samaria"
- v. 10 [of antithetic], "they all gave heed, from the least to the greatest"
- v. 12, "they ... men and women were baptized"
- v. 14, "the apostles ... heard that Samaria had received the word of God."

The opposite is the case of Philip's conversation with the Ethiopian Eunuch, who we assume from the text of Scripture, was not traveling alone: the Holy Spirit constantly emphasized singularity in this conversation:

- v. 27, "a man"
- v. 28, "sitting in his chariot, he was reading"
- v. 30, "Philip ran to him, and heard him reading"
- v. 30, "Do you [singular] understand what you [singular] are reading?"
- v. 31, "And he said, 'How can I, unless, unless someone guides me?'"
- v. 31, "And he asked Phillip to come up and sit with him"
- v. 32, "He read"
- v. 34, "I ask you"
- v. 35, "Philip opened his mouth, and beginning at this Scripture, preached Jesus to him."

It isn't until verse 36 that there is the plural form found, "Now as they went down the road." And the singular continues with this wonderful example of believer's baptism by immersion in the Book of Acts.

The Holy Spirit made it imminently clear that it is not a matter of either/or, but both/and! The Bible keeps mass evangelism in balance with personal evangelism. The two remain together in perfect synergy: both are equally vital and necessary.

Before this methodological shift fully took hold in the North, Southern Baptist evangelists began to organize for evangelism!

- **Southern Baptists Organize as Evangelists**

C. E. Matthews came to the Home Mission Board from Texas, where he had successfully led that state in evangelism, particularly organizing simultaneous revivals in Texas cities. For example, in Dallas on March 23-April 6, 1947, 86 Baptist churches cooperated to conduct a simultaneous revival during the same week. The poster read, "Attend the friendly Baptist Church in your neighborhood."[11] This same organizational talent and enthusiasm was brought to Atlanta, and placed at the service of the entire SBC. The result were God-blessed years of harvest for Southern Baptists.

Table 3 illustrates the number of recorded Baptisms in SBC churches from 1900 to 2007. It is clear from this chart that the first spike of growth took place when there was a discussion of a Department of Evangelism between 1904 and 1906. Hamilton's stable of salaried evangelists, preaching localized simultaneous revivals, was effective. Then another spike took place in the late 1940s and early 1950s. This second spike was related to the leadership of C. E. Matthews and the nationwide simultaneous revivals that he and his network of forty associates organized and encouraged.[12] J. N. Barnette's ambitious program of Sunday School recruitment is remembered by the phrase, "A Million More in '54." It appears that the shadow left by C. E. Matthews (with the help of J. N. Barnett) indelibly marked the pattern for future simultaneous

---

[11]Ibid., poster insert on back flap.

[12]"The staff of the evangelism department remained small, yet through the network he created, Matthews actually had more people working with him than earlier secretaries with a staff of more than forty evangelists and singers" (Kelley, *How Did They Do It?*, 35).

TABLE 3: Baptisms and Simultaneous Revival Evangelism

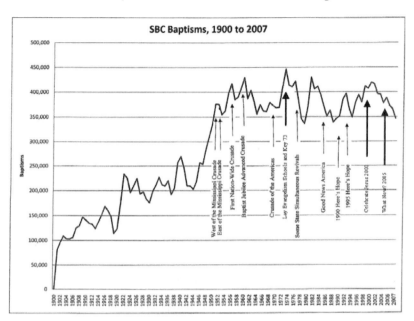

revivals, as well as for the directorship of the Department of Evangelism.

The dates and names of some of the simultaneous revivals are listed on the chart (1956, 1960, 1970, 1973, 1986, 1990, 1995, 2000, 2005). These revivals needed at least a three year preparation time in order for proper communication of its name, date, and goals. For example, the recent simultaneous revival, "Celebrate Jesus 2000," had success in baptisms from 1997 to 1999, even though it had reduced funding. Its synergy created a wave of baptisms. The historic events on "9-11" (2001) also resulted in a spike of baptisms in 2001 and 2002. However, the simultaneous revival called "What Now? 2005" suffered from last-minute defunding and a lack of unified administration.

Whatever the case, when simultaneous revivals were encouraged, multiple evangelists needed to be available during the same week of meetings. This need for and use of independently-funded evangelists fostered a grassroots environment that honored the office of the evangelist and encouraged young men to enter into the ministry.

Simultaneously, the SBC seminaries were going through theological stresses. Leaders like R. G. Lee were seeking to foster revival within SBC churches. The Baptist Faith and Message was revised in 1963 to shore up SBC theology. Meanwhile, not all seminaries appeared to encourage or promote revival evangelism and the use of evangelists.

However, a third movement was taking place—that of the organizing of Southern Baptist Evangelists into COSBE (Conference of Southern Baptist Evangelists) in 1958. Thirty-two men gathered Wednesday evening during the SBC meeting in Houston to found an Evangelists' Conference, much like there was a Pastors' Conference. The speakers were Robert Witty and Evangelist E. J. Daniels. The purpose of this early group was explained in its Constitution:

> "The purpose of this conference is to promote fellowship among those engaged in evangelism among Southern Baptist Churches and to provide inspiration and information to assist the evangelist to better serve the Lord Jesus Christ and the churches among whom they minister."[13]

The membership was to be made up of the following:

> "The membership of this conference shall be composed of members of Southern Baptist Churches who are certified as messengers to the Southern Baptist Convention by their respective churches and who devote their lives to the service of Jesus Christ, the Son of the Living God as occupational evangelists, commonly known as General Evangelists, Singer Evangelists, Denominational Workers who serve Southern Baptist Churches as Evangelists, and Southern Baptist Pastors, Educational Directors, and Ministers of Music who devote a portion of their time as Pastor-Evangelist"[14]

---

[13]Fordham, *The Evangelist: Born in the Heart of God*; unpublished manuscript, 2009.
[14]Ibid.

At the second meeting, Evangelist Mordecai Ham spoke, and the group consisted of about 100 people, many of whom were not evangelists. Sometimes COSBE was guided by such pastors as R. G. Lee (serving as president of the Conference one year), and missionaries like W. H. Jackson and C. E. Autrey of the Home Mission Board. The Wednesday meetings grew every year. By 1965 there were 4,000 present at the Evangelists' Conference. Evangelist Don Womack stated, "Reports began to pour in from all over the Convention of the blessing of the Evangelists' Conference."[15]

Broadman began publishing the programs for the Evangelists' Conference in 1966. This practice continued until 1974. By that time the number of evangelists in the membership of COSBE grew from 35-40 to 350-400. In 1973, the COSBE's Constitution was updated. Its purposes were expanded to include four main points:

> "This organization shall serve as a tool, both for the individual evangelist and the Southern Baptist Convention as a whole, to spread the gospel of Jesus Christ thus, its purpose shall be:
>
> "1. Fellowship among its members and with all other individuals in the Lord.
>
> "2. Offer to its members a means of expressing the convictions of the conference to the Southern Baptist Convention and to a lost world.
>
> "3. Provide opportunity for the evangelists to be a yearly source of inspiration to pastors and laymen of the Southern Baptist Convention.
>
> "4. Act as a teaching instrument—sharing with the convention and pastors the ministry and gift of the evangelist, according to Eph. 4:11— thus, fulfilling the Great Commission."[16]

In 1968, Evangelist Bob Harrington invited the conference of evangelists and musicians to participate in a revival to be held at the Show-Bar Nightclub during the SBC in New Orleans.[17] This became what was called the "Stalnecker Open House," funded by Evangelist Charles Massagee and hosted by Evangelist Ed and Bette Stalnecker after the evening sessions of the SBC, from 10 pm until midnight.

[15]Ibid.
[16]Ibid.
[17]John Scott Trent, *Evangelists in Action*, 44.

During these meetings, which spanned over two decades, Music Evangelists had the opportunity to sing before pastors and messengers.

Later, in 1998, Jerry Drace, President of COSBE initiated the Sunday morning Evangelists Worship Service, to replace the Wednesday evening service that dwindled when the SBC schedule was shortened.

In 1969 a Directory of Evangelists was published by Charles Massagee. He explained:

> "When I was elected president in 1969, I took it on myself to publish the first directory. I printed 50,000 copies. We made 25,000 available at the SBC in 1970 and mailed 25,000 copies to pastors. I paid for the printing, and then I wrote everyone to send me $30 to help with the expense, and they did."[18]

During Massagee's presidency of COSBE, they also began taking dues, primarily funding the directory. Some State Conventions have State Conference of Evangelists which also have sent out directories at various times: Florida, Georgia, Missouri, Tennessee, Texas, and others. With the use of simultaneous revivals and growth in the number of evangelists, membership qualifications for COSBE were also adapted in 1973. Membership was limited to full-time vocational evangelists, with non-full-time evangelists being considered for "Honorary Membership." The qualifications included procedures for joining, membership dues, and establishing a Central Office. A member of COSBE since 1961, Evangelist Don Womack was made the permanent Secretary-Treasurer (Executive Director) in 1973.

In 1975 Bobby Sunderland joined the Home Mission Board (HMB) in part to be a liaison between the HMB and COSBE. That same year a special retreat for Southern Baptist evangelists was held at Southwest Baptist College in Bolivar, Missouri. This conference was a God-send for Keith Fordham and his wife Shirley, as they

---

[18]Charles Massagee, from personal email to Keith Fordham, 6 Aug 2012.

were just entering the ministry of full-time vocational evangelism. Through the years, the HMB (now North American Mission Board) has assisted the evangelists in the following ways:

- Hosted the COSBE retreat the weekend prior to the SBC, providing lodging, meals, training, and fellowship for COSBE members;
- Printed and distributed the *Directory of Vocational Southern Baptist Evangelists*;
- Provided space for a COSBE booth at the SBC
- Provided revival preparation manuals
- Instituted a "Low or No Baptism" program, which became the "Baptismal Assistance Program" to assist evangelists who preach a churches
- Subsidized the transportation, lodging, and meals for COSBE officers to attend various NAMB meetings.

Toby Frost became NAMB's COSBE liaison in 2000. He served in that role until 2005. He also blessed the evangelists with encouragement, resources, and fellowship opportunities.

- **Fellowship among SBC Evangelists**

Yet, even with all these opportunities, just as Elijah, the vocational evangelists can grow lonely as he and his wife and family minister the gospel from one church to another, week in and week out. Fellowship with other evangelists is vital.

Along with fellowship comes mentoring. Many young evangelists do not make it in the ministry because they receive no mentoring. Often they do not know where to look, nor to whom they should look, for encouragement. So an important need that COSBE fills is to provide "iron sharpens iron" opportunities for all evangelists, and especially young evangelists entering the ministry. Because most seminaries are not very well-equipped to provide this type of training, COSBE can provide the necessary "on the job" training.

Some have looked to COSBE to be a "Clearing House" for evangelists, and it does function in that role. It also has a disciplinary function. Yet, providing preventive maintenance is usually much less costly than providing emergency care.

If the Lord is calling you into full-time vocational evangelism, contact an evangelist and tell him. Contact the State Director of Evangelism, and ask him for suggestions. Join the conference of evangelists in your state convention. Join COSBE and attend their meetings, even if you have to sacrifice to do so. If your seminary offers a class on the "Work of the Evangelist," please take that class.

If Elijah, a man who met with Jesus at the Transfiguration (Matt 17:3; Mark 9:4), went through discouragement. We can be sure that we will also face discouragement. Rather, let's avail ourselves of the fellowship of the saints, and press on to fulfill the Great Commission.

CHAPTER TWO

THE ROLE OF THE EVANGELIST

*"The Purpose of the Conference of Southern Baptist Evangelists has been
to encourage Bible preaching, gospel singing, and personal witnessing.
These are the endeavors that have strengthened Southern Baptists when
other denominations have moved away from these fundamentals and
weakened their position."*

Robert G. Lee

There are three uses of the word "evangelist" in the New
Testament. Yet, interestingly, these uses are three times more than
the New Testament's use of the word "pastor." The New Testament
uses the word pastor only once in Ephesians 4:11, the same verse
that also lists the evangelist as a leader in the church. However, just
as a pastor is important to the local church, so it appears that the
evangelist has a role in the local church.

Now, it must be admitted and affirmed up front that a positive
view of an evangelist is derived from a specific view of conversion.
That is, that personal faith comes by hearing the Gospel proclaimed,
that the Holy Spirit accompanies the Word of God, and gives a
hearing of faith to some, and that the individual soul is free to
respond to the Gospel when it is heard. Therefore, the focus of the
evangelist is on the proclamation of the Word of God in such a way
as to focus on the Gospel and on the conversion of his hearers. Yet
most theological approaches to salvation and conversion confuse this
simple work, often leaving out the need for an evangelist in the
process. So, it is important for the reader to understand up front how
volatile this subject is, and in particular, how volatile the role of the
evangelist is, due to his focus on one method, type, and style of
conversion: hearing and believing!

22

How does the work of an evangelist relate to the work of a pastor? Is there not some overlap? Yes, there is. While some pastors do not see their roles as relating at all to the work of an evangelist, others see evangelism as their primary focus. Yet in God's providence, He has laid a special call on some men in His church to keep its evangelism activity alive and well. These men He called "evangelists."

In order to best understand the place of the evangelist in Christ's church, this chapter will be divided into two sections. The first section will consider some definitions of the evangelist. While not having the authority of Scripture, these definitions will help the reader to understand how some men have defined the role of the evangelist, and therefore place the evangelist within a historical and methodological context. Next, we will look at Scripture, seeking a definitive definition of the role and place of the evangelist. Where modern definitions can sometimes seem tedious and contradictory, the New Testament dispels any doubts as to the role and place of the evangelist.

Noah Webster, Jr., graduate of Yale in 1778 and American lexicographer, defined the term "evangelist" in this way, "One who travels from place to place particularly as a preacher; one who is unsettled." It must also be noted that Webster also published a revision of the King James Bible in 1833, and was therefore very well aware of the biblical record on this subject. His basic definition has been followed by others.[1]

John Bunyan, author of *Pilgrim's Progress*, explained the role of the evangelist early in that work. Bunyan described "Evangelist" using the voice of "Interpreter" as he explained a portrait of "Evangelist" to the main character in the book, "Christian":

> "'The man, whose picture this is,' said the Interpreter, 'is one of a thousand. I have shown you his picture first of all, because the man

---

[1] J. Vernon McGee, *Exploring Through Ephesians* (Laverne, California: El Camino Press, n.d.), 56; *Wuest's Word Studies: Ephesians and Colossians* (Grand Rapids: Eerdmans, 1953), 1:100-01.

whose picture this is, is the only man who the Lord of the place whither thou art going hath authorized to be thy guide.'

"Christian, gazing at the picture, saw, as Bunyan describes, 'A man, who has his eyes up to heaven, the best of books was in his hand, the law of truth was written upon his lips, and he stood as if he pleaded with men.'"[2]

Bisagno emphasized the evangelist's God-given ability to draw the net:

"When a man is the gift of God [evangelist] to the church he has the ability to present the facts of the gospel in order to persuade men to turn to Christ. His main ability is to draw the net when he gives an invitation. In short, he can get a man to 'sign on the dotted line' for Christ."[3]

Delos Miles described the Evangelist in this way:

"An evangelist is a Christian specially called by God and supernaturally gifted by the Holy Spirit to break up some new ground or to claim some new territory for the Lord Jesus Christ.

"Philip, one of the seven in Acts 6, is 'Exhibit A' of a Biblical evangelist (see Acts 6:5; 21:8; 8:4-40). Timothy is an example of one instructed to 'do the work of an evangelist' (2 Tim 4:5). Evangelists (along with apostles, prophets, pastors and teachers) are called and gifted to equip God's people for the work of ministry, 'for building up the body of Christ' internally and externally (see Eph 4:11-16)."[4]

Therefore, from these four definitions some preliminary conclusions can be drawn. Webster chose to focus his definition on the movement of the evangelist. Bunyan focused on the evangelist's role in leading people to salvation in Jesus Christ. Bisagno focused on the ability to draw the net. Miles saw the evangelist as a pioneer church planter, and then he looked at Scripture to consider the three passages where the word "evangelist" is used.

---

[2] James A. Stewart, *Invasion of Wales by the Spirit* (Fort Washington, PN: Christian Literature Crusade, n.d.), 68.

[3] John Bisagno, interview with Keith Fordham, Georgia Evangelism Conference, Savannah, GA (21 Jan 1987).

[4] Delos Miles. Personal letter to Keith Fordham. n.d.

gospel and conversion. Paul wanted Timothy to "do the work of an evangelist."

It is very interesting that the clearest call to the ministry of the evangelist in the New Testament is not given directly to evangelists, but rather to pastors. Christ obviously knew the reproach of the gospel, and also the likelihood that pastors would drift away from doing evangelism. The drift away from evangelism is proven throughout history.

Yet, in calling Timothy to do the work of an evangelist, it appears that an example of an evangelist needed to be both in Paul's mind, in the mind of Timothy, and in the mind of the Holy Spirit. While we cannot get into the mind of Paul, unless he specifically stated it, nor can we get in the mind of Timothy, we do have an example of an evangelist under the inspiration of the Holy Spirit—a fine example of the clarity and sufficiency of the Word of God! God gave us an example of the work of an evangelist through the ministry of Philip in Acts 8. The reason that we can say this with strong assurance is that Philip is the only person in Scripture specifically called an evangelist, as found in Acts 21:8. Now there are several aspects of the ministry of Philip developed in Acts. First, in Acts 6 we have the spiritual and ministry qualifications of the evangelist. Second, we have the "work of the evangelist" exemplified in Acts 8.

So then, who is qualified to be an evangelist? Three qualifications are listed in Acts 6:3. They are to be "men of [good] reputation, full of the Holy Spirit and wisdom." The word "good" in the translation is implied before the word "reputation." Therefore, the evangelist should not be a man with a tarnished reputation. They need to be full of the Holy Spirit, which also implies that they are filled with the Word of God, which is the sword of the Spirit (Eph 6:17). Further they are to be filled with wisdom. This latter may explain why Southern Baptists tend to appreciate evangelists who have the experience of age, as age tends to allow time for the nurture of wisdom.

But what do we learn about the work of an evangelist from Acts 8. Interestingly, we can learn a lot. First of all, it appears that the Holy Spirit shows that all true disciples were to proclaim the Word of God. In Acts 8:4, all those who were scattered, "went everywhere preaching the word." Therefore, the work of evangelism is not a unique role or responsibility for the evangelist alone. Evangelism is the responsibility of all God's children. Every true believer must confess and keep confessing Christ before men in order for Christ to confess him before the Father:

- Matt 10:32, "Therefore whoever confesses Me before men, him I will also confess before My Father who is in heaven" (cf. Luke 12:8)

And the opposite is also true:

- Mark 8:38, "For whoever is ashamed of Me and My words in this adulterous and sinful generation, of him the Son of Man also will be ashamed when He comes in the glory of His Father with the holy angels" (cf. Luke 9:26).

So it is clear that all of God's people must be about the business of confessing Christ before men.[5]

However, the evangelist, just like Philip, has a special calling in that area. While he was married with children, and owned a home in Caesarea (Acts 21:8-9), his evangelism ministry brought him to the ancient capital city of the northern tribes of Israel, the city of Samaria.

A brief word about the verbs used in Acts 8:4-5. In Acts 8:4, the text says, "those who were scattered went everywhere preaching the word." The word for "preaching" in the Greek is *euangelizo*, or in English "evangelize." They were "evangelizing" with the content of their preaching being "the word." As for Philip in Acts 8:5, he went

---

[5]C. C. Randall, former Professor of Evangelism at NOBTS, rightly wrote: "All Christians are to be witnesses. All Christians are to be evangelistic even though, in the biblical sense, all are not called to be evangelists. While every sermon preached is not to be an evangelistic sermon, each one must contain the evangel or it cannot be called a Christian message" (C. C. Randall. Personal letter to Keith Fordham. n.d.).

down to the city of Samaria and preached Christ to them. In this case, the word for "preached" in the Greek is *kerusso*. Philip was heralding the message of the gospel about "Christ." So notice that the special word "evangelize" from which is derived the term "evangelist" was used in this case not of the "evangelist," but rather for all the scattered disciples.

Further, as the ministry of Philip the Evangelist is introduced in Acts 8, so is the carnal ministry of Simon the Sorcerer. Luke appears to introduce them using the powerful tool of antithetic parallelism. Both Philip and Simon had the entire town as their audience. Both Philip and Simon were heeded by the whole town. But the focus of their ministry was entirely different, as was the final result. One preached himself, the other Christ; one brought astonishment, the other joy. Table 4 seeks to portray some of these differences.

Could it be that the ministries of some evangelists can morph into a self-centered ministry, just as that of Simon the Sorcerer? The Holy Spirit provides a solemn example and warning even as He introduces the role and ministry of the evangelist.

Now, Philip has a city-wide harvest evangelism ministry in Samaria. Yet, in the second part of Acts 8, he also shows a willingness to be involved in personal evangelism. Often so-called "mass evangelism" and "personal evangelism" can be seen to be at odds one with another. Those who favor one will sometimes denigrate those who do the other. In this case, Philip is an example of both-and. God the Holy Spirit superintended that both personal and mass evangelism were a part of his ministry example as documented in the Bible.

The interim between Philip's ministry in Samaria and with the Ethiopian Eunuch contains several nuggets. Several other uses of the verb "evangelize" are found in this interesting chapter. The second use of this verb is found in describing the ministry of Philip in Acts 8:12. Philip was "evangelizing," then some people "believed," and following their profession of faith, he "baptized" them. So Philip the evangelist was evangelizing, and also baptizing! In Acts 8:25 we

TABLE 4: Carnal and Spiritual Evangelists Compared

	Philip the Evangelist	Simon the Sorcerer	Similar/ Different
Summary	A Preacher ——— A Spiritual Ministry	An Entertainer ——— A Carnal Ministry	Different
Ministry	Evangelist, 21:8	Practicing magic, 8:9	Different
Method	Proclaiming, 8:5 Included verbal (hearing) and healings (saw signs), 8:6-7, 13 Preaching, 8:12	Practicing magic, 8:9 His magic arts, 8:11	Different
Length of ministry	[short time]	Long time, 8:11	Different
Message	Christ, 8:5 Kingdom of God and the name of Jesus Christ, 8:12	Claiming to be someone great, 8:9 "This man is the called the Great Power of God," 8:10	Different
Focus of Message	Christ	Simon himself	Different
Audience	The crowds with one accord, 8:6 City, 8:8 Men and women, 8:12	The people of Samaria, 8:9 Smallest to greatest, 8:10	Same
Appeal	Giving attention, 8:6	Giving attention, 8:10, 11	Same
Signs	Performed signs, 8:6; cast out unclean spirits, paralyzed and lame healed, 8:7; signs and great miracles, 8:13	Magic arts, 8:11	Different
Result of ministry	Rejoicing, 8:8	Astonishment, 8:9	Different

have the Apostles Peter and John "evangelizing." Evangelizing was therefore not below the pay grade or spiritual rank of the apostles. Then in Acts 8:35, Philip is again "evangelizing," but this time he was "evangelizing Jesus" to him. Finally in Acts 8:40 we have the fifth and final use of the Greek verb *euaggelizo* in Acts 8, again referring to the ministry of Philip, evangelizing as he headed back home to Samaria. So, to summarize, the verb "evangelize" is used of Philip three times, of all the disciples once, and of the apostle Peter and John once. These uses include everyone in the church—every member evangelism!

When Philip entered Samaria to preach the Gospel, Jesus had been nearby just a few short years earlier. Jesus determined to go through Samaria, where he led the Woman at the Well to Himself. She then led many people from her own town, more of whom were saved when Jesus stayed among them.

- "And many of the Samaritans of that city believed in Him because of the word of the woman who testified, 'He told me all that I *ever* did.' So when the Samaritans had come to Him, they urged Him to stay with them; and He stayed there two days. And many more believed because of His own word. Then they said to the woman, 'Now we believe, not because of what you said, for we ourselves have heard *Him* and we know that this is indeed the Christ, the Savior of the world.'" (John 4:39-42)

So Jesus seeded the region of the Samaritans prior to the arrival of Philip. Philip then followed up on that area already seeded by the Savior, and leading to a work of God in Samaria.

As to Philip and the Ethiopian Eunuch, we find Philip leaving a bona fide revival, because he felt compelled to go to a certain place on a desert road. When he arrived, God placed a man in his path who was reading Isaiah 53, the prophecy about the Substitutionary death of Jesus. Now isn't that a great Holy Ghost prepared event! Also, although there is more than just the Ethiopian Eunuch in the entourage, as it was unlikely that the Eunuch was reading aloud while driving a carriage (my wife sometimes gets on me for that). Luke, however, focuses only on the two directly engaged in the conversation, much like he does in Acts 26, when Felix and Agrippa are in the audience, along with many other people (Acts 25:23). The common order of events in the salvation of an individual, already noted in Acts 8:12, occurs again. The Ethiopian Eunuch hears the Gospel, he believes, and he is baptized. Notice, that in the often excluded verse, Acts 8:37, the Eunuch is baptized based on his own verbal profession of faith, "Then Philip said, 'If you believe with all your heart, you may.' And he answered and said, 'I believe that Jesus Christ is the Son of God'" (Acts 8:37).

Another point comes to the fore, Acts 8 provides us one of the clearest examples of believers baptism in the New Testament. He was really saved before he was baptized. He was not an infant, nor was he saved because of, by, or after he was baptized. He was saved before he was baptized. Nor did he speak in tongues as part of his baptism. Remembering the importance of Acts 15:7-11, with its allusion to the events that transpired in Acts 10:44-48, even those of household of Cornelius were completely saved before they were baptized. How do we know? Because they spoke in tongues by the Holy Spirit! And Ephesians 1:13, shows that after we believe, we are sealed with the Holy Spirit of promise. Those of the household of Cornelius were saved and sealed, proving that they were ready for the water.

A last surprising truth associated with the Ethiopian Eunuch, Philip the Evangelist did not do follow-up on the Eunuch—the Holy Spirit did. He was on both sides of the equation, preparation and follow-up. In preparation, the Holy Spirit was working through the words of Isaiah 53. Then, the follow-up on the Eunuch was done by the Holy Spirit. And part of that was through the Word of God, with which he was already becoming familiar. In Acts 8:39 we read, "the Spirit of the Lord caught Philip away." So Philip's removal was not his fault, nor was it his choice or prerogative. The Spirit of the Lord caught him away. And the Eunuch went on his way rejoicing, much like those in the city of Samaria (Acts 8:7), and those in Antioch when Paul and Barnabas were forcibly removed from the city (Acts 13:52). So, while evangelists are often accused of having no concern for follow-up, perhaps it would be wise for those who throw such epithets to first consider the text of Scripture on this matter.

Two further questions emanate from the example of Philip in Acts 8. One, what is the special leadership role of the evangelist that sets him apart from the pastor or teacher? And two, how then can and ought a local pastor do the "work of an evangelist"?

From the earlier listed definitions of evangelists, four points come forth that appear to distinguish his ministry. Let's consider these four and several others to see which of these is unique to the evangelist:

- A traveling or itinerating ministry (Webster)
- A pioneer ministry (Miles)
- Ability to draw the net (Bisagno)
- A unique focus on conversion (Bunyan)

- A harvesting where preparation had been done (as in the case of Philip's ministry)
- A baptizing of new believers into the church.

Certainly, Philip in Acts 8 certainly had an itinerating ministry. Philip also appears to have had a pioneering ministry. Philip preached in a compelling way, which led the Eunuch to the point of conversion, affirmed through profession followed by baptism. But perhaps most importantly, Philip's ministry was one devoted to evangelizing about Christ and the conversion of souls. Let's, therefore, expound on these and compare the ministry of a pastor with that of an evangelist (see Table 5).

Of the six points brought up in Table 4, out of the six categories, 3 of the 6 are clearly different. The pastor has a stationary ministry, he ministers where a church has already been planted, he shepherds the flock of God, and his ministry focus is inside the church. The pastor is also to do the work of an evangelist outside the church. The evangelist, however, has an itinerating ministry, sometimes he ministers where churches are not yet established, his focus is also both inside and outside the church, on reaching lost souls with the gospel. The similarity between evangelists and pastors: they both need to preach Christ crucified. Lastly, is the ability to draw the net. Some pastors are gifted in giving invitations, but as mentioned by Bisagno, giving a proper gospel appeal is a part of the special calling of the evangelist.

If this is truly the case, then, how can a pastor "do the work evangelist"? Is he to begin itinerating? Not necessarily. It appears that he is to imitate the evangelist in keeping an outward evangelistic focus as part of his ministry. His "doing the work of an evangelist" ought to lead him to appreciate and value the ministry of the evangelist. He will invite the evangelist and prepare for upcoming revivals in his church. He will be going outside the four walls of the church to evangelize. It may mean doing pioneer ministry (church planting) or sending others to unreached areas (missions). Perhaps the best example of the need for this outward focus is found in the

TABLE 5: Evangelist and Pastor Compared

	Evangelist	Pastor	Similar/ Different
Movement	Traveling or itinerating	Stationary	Different
Pioneer focus	Both where the church is already established or where Christ has not been named	Where the church is already established	Similar/ Different
Revivalism	Where the church is established, emphasizing commitment	Where the church is established, leading his people to commitment	Similar
Ministry focus	Reach lost souls, bring them to Christ	Shepherding the flock of God	Different
Relation to church	Outside and inside the church	Outside and inside the church	Similar
Message	Jesus, the Gospel, Christ	Jesus, the Gospel, Christ	Similar
Invitation	Ability to draw the net	Must preach Jesus passionately	Similar/ Different

words of God to Paul in a dream in Acts 18:9-10. In these verses, God had to tell Paul to stop his itinerating for a while and to stay in Corinth, in order to reach the people of that area:

- Acts 18:9-10, "Now the Lord spoke to Paul in the night by a vision, 'Do not be afraid, but speak, and do not keep silent; for I am with you, and no one will attack you to hurt you; for I have many people in this city.'"

Here in this case, rather than itinerate to reach more souls, God called on Paul to stay in Corinth, and to keep evangelizing ("speak, and do not keep silent"). Therefore, effective evangelistic ministry does not have to be itinerating, nor does it have to be pioneer ministry. A pastor can and ought to reach the city where he is located, because there are many lost people in that city also. God wanted Paul to keep an outward focus on the lost people in the city of Corinth, even though a body of believers was beginning to gather as a result of his evangelism ministry. Perhaps reaching outside the four walls of the church is the best way that a pastor can, "Do the work of an evangelist."

In similar way, church planters are also doing the work of an evangelist in pioneer areas. They are claiming new spiritual territory for the Lord. May each be careful how he builds (1 Cor 3:10). So using the rubric of Acts 8 and 18 to define the ministry of the evangelist, church planting is doing the work of an evangelist and is essentially pioneer evangelism, like that of Philip and Paul.

Whatever the case, it is clear that the focus of the evangelist is on the Evangel, the gospel, and on getting that gospel to those who have not yet heard or received Christ. He must be willing to go wherever and whenever the Lord calls. The centrality of his ministry makes the evangelist the example for the pastor. John R. Rice understood the importance of the work of the evangelist:

> "The work of evangelism is preeminently the central task of Christianity. Evangelism is the heart of the Great Commission. The evangelist, that is, the man who wins souls and teaches and inspires others to win souls, is the closest to the center of the will of God."[6]

Not only is the work of the evangelist to be central in the heart and mind of the evangelist. The work of the evangelist is to be central in the heart and mind of the pastor. Evangelists have more than a mere peripheral role in the church, their role is exemplary. It is front and center in keeping the church on target with Christ's Great Commission. So Carroll rightly cried out for evangelists: "Give me evangelists!"

Evangelists were needed in the 20th Century, and they are still the real need in 21st Century!

---

[6]John R. Rice, *The Evangelist and His Work* (Murfreesboro: Sword of the Lord, 1968), 19.

The WORTH AND WORK OF THE EVANGELIST

CHAPTER THREE

THE FIVE-FOLD MINISTRY AND TYPES OF EVANGELISTS

"The bedrock of Scripture underlies it. Experience demonstrates its wisdom and feasibility. If the Home Mission Board may employ any man, it may employ evangelists. Altogether, then, with a ring, let us support this measure. If I were the secretary of the board I would come before this body in humility and tears and say: 'Brethren, give me evangelists. Deny not fins to things that must swim against the tide, nor wings to things that must fly against the wind.'"

B. H. Carroll [1906]

Just as evangelists were needed in 1906, so they are still needed today. But what is meant when the word "evangelist" is used? In Chapter Two we noted that the office of evangelist is different from the office of the pastor in at least four ways: involves itineration, includes pioneer work, focus on lost souls inside and outside the church, and includes the divine gift to give an appeal. Yet these four distinctions also necessitate further expansion on the possibility of differing types of evangelists. In another chapter we will note the absolute necessity of the evangelist being in relationship with a local church. In this chapter we look at types of evangelists beginning with their relationship to what is sometimes called the "five-fold ministry" of Ephesians 4:11.

If the esteemed reader would like to consider the five-fold ministry as found in Ephesians 4:11 as a present reality, then the following may be considered. The apostle is, generally speaking, a "sent one." He is not to be considered as one who speaks with "apostolic authority" as used by Paul in 2 Cor 12:12. Rather the emphasis is in a practical sense as a missionary or "sent one" into another region or culture. The missionary is sent by a church in one locality and/or culture and into another locality and/or culture. Further, as a pioneer missionary, this type of "sent one" is by necessity both a "sent one" and an "evangelist."

The prophet, for his part, may be considered a revivalist. The prophet's primary ministry in the Old and New Testaments was to the people of God. The prophet called God's people back to God, just as the revivalist's ministry is to call God's people back to God.

The evangelist's ministry is focused on the lost inside and outside the church. He is especially called to evangelize the lost. He tells people about Jesus and incites Christians to share the gospel. While a part of the church, his role is focused on those outside of Christ. The evangelist's focus within the church is exemplified in being a divinely mandated charge to pastors that they "Do the work of an evangelist" (2 Tim 4:5). Anyone finding themselves in Ephesians 4:11 as a teacher must also "Do the work of an evangelist." Not only ought the teacher himself do the work of an evangelist, but he must focus his classes and lectures on leading and teaching his students to do the same. He is no Great Commission professor, who does not teach with the work of the evangelist in the forefront of his mind! This missional interpretation is only logical if we are to uphold a Great Commission church.

Now, how do these five leaders in the church coalesce around Matthew's Great Commission? Matthew 28:19-20 includes four commands: (1-2) go and win disciples; (3) baptize the won disciples; and (4) teach the won and baptized disciples to obey. The following provides a hybridization of Matthew 28:19-20 with the five leaders mentioned in Ephesians 4:11.

In a Great Commission centered interpretation of the five leaders in Ephesians 4:11, the "apostles" or pioneer missionaries and "evangelists" are focused on going and winning disciples. Both are going. The pioneer missionary is sent to people in cross-cultural settings, whereas the evangelist is generally sent to lost peoples and populations within his same language and culture. Both the pioneer missionary and the evangelist are called to win disciples. The other three Ephesians 4 leaders, revivalist, the pastor, and the teacher, are focused on equipping God's people. The "prophets" or revivalists keep the hearts of God's people stirred to Great Commission action. "Pastors" shepherd the flock of God over whom they are made overseers. It is pastors and local churches who generally baptize the newly won disciples. The teachers then confirm, affirm, and follow-up on the ministry of the four others. They are to teach God's people to observe all things that Christ commanded them, including the "go and win disciples" of the Great Commission. It is a sad day when teachers pull the hearts of God's people away from the work of the pioneer missionary, the revivalist, and the evangelist.

But yet another distinction needs to be made. When defining the position and role of the evangelist, it must be remembered from the outset, "If everybody is an evangelist, then no one is an evangelist." Therefore, while every disciple of Christ is to evangelize, not every disciple of Christ is an Ephesians 4:11 leader-evangelist. So, W. B. Riley was correct in one sense when he wrote that every convert to Christ is a commissioned evangelist:

> "Every true convert to Christ is a commissioned evangelist.... The method of the Wesleyans was in perfect accord with the prescription of the Word; and was equally adapted to the eighteenth, nineteenth, or twentieth century—'All at it: always at it'—every convert to Christ a commissioned Evangelist."[1]

Yet there is a distinction between the Ephesians 4:11 leader-evangelist that Christ has given to the church and every true member of the church. Riley was seeking to rally the Northern Baptist churches of the early 20th Century to refocus on evangelizing. He was emphasizing that all Christians ought to be involved in winning souls to Christ.

Evangelist Jesse Hendley made the distinction involved clear:

---

[1]W. B. Riley, *The Crisis of the Church* (New York: Charles C. Cook, 1914), 79, 80.

"The person God uses for revival must be called of God for this work. 'And no man takes this honor to himself, but he who is called by God,' (Heb 5:4).

"All true believers are 'called saints,' that is, are saints by divine and personal call and are called to witness and to win souls. But Evangelists are Christ's gifts to the church for soul winning revivals (Eph 4:11), and they obtain this office by divine call! Paul was 'a called apostle' (Rom 1:1, Greek), called to the specific work of reaching the Gentiles. Even Christ was *'called of God as high priest'* (Heb 5:10). Out of the original seven who were chosen by the early church to serve tables, only Philip was called 'the Evangelist' (Acts 21:8). The others were not so called. Evidently God called him to this work after his call to serve tables. Paul urged Timothy to *'do the work of an Evangelist'* (2 Tim 4:5). He did not urge him to leave his charge and go out from place to place for revivals as called Evangelists did, but as a pastor-teacher to promote revival and soul winning on his field between the comings of the Evangelists! He was to keep the fires of evangelism blazing all the time! But he was not set apart by God and gifted for that special work of the Evangelist. His special call was to teach (2 Tim 2:2)."[2]

While there is a role for the pastor in evangelism, while there is a role for the Christian in evangelism, God has a special role for His evangelist. The evangelist is a God-called leader that Christ gave His local church to focus exclusively on preaching revivals, evangelizing the lost, and training the church to evangelize the lost. In so doing, a blessed by-product of submission to the leadership of the evangelist is God's protection over the Great Commission doctrines of the local church.

As we discuss ten specific types of evangelists, we begin with what we call "four biblical types of evangelists." We call them biblical, due to the analysis of these types with the other leaders mentioned in Ephesians 4.

---

[2]Jesse Hendley, "The Only Person God Can Use for Revival," in Robert J. Wells and John R. Rice, eds. *How To Have Revival by America's Leading Evangelists* (Wheaton: Sword of the Lord, 1946), 111.

- **Four biblical types of evangelists**

The first four types of evangelists are derived from a Great Commission interpretation of the five leaders listed in Ephesians 4:11. They are preaching evangelists, revivalists, pioneer missionaries, and church planters. These four types of evangelists are foundational for our further discussion on types of evangelists. It is our wish, that as you read these descriptors, that God the Holy Spirit will be clarifying His calling in your life, dear reader.

- ○ **Preaching evangelists**

Preaching evangelists, constitute the largest and most prominent type of evangelists. When the word "evangelist" is used, most often people think of the preaching evangelist. Keith Fordham is an example of a preaching evangelist. He travels from church to church, upon the request of a pastor, and preaches a series of meetings at the church generally called "revivals." His passion is two-fold, to call lost people to faith in Jesus Christ and to awaken the saints to the need for evangelism. He reminds us that evangelism and revival go hand in hand. The Conference of Southern Baptist Evangelists (COSBE) is made up of a large number of men, most of whom are preaching evangelists.

Billy Graham and Greg Laurie are also prominent examples of preaching evangelists. They emphasize city-wide crusades. Their goal is to organize multiple churches in one city to have a crusade or festival in one venue (such as a civic auditorium or sports arena). The added complexity in their ministry is that of making decisions regarding cooperative evangelism among churches of various denominations and other religious groupings.

- ○ **Revivalists**

The revivalist has a parallel ministry to that of the preaching evangelist. While not specifically an "evangelist," his calling may approximate that of a "prophet" in Ephesians 4:11. In the contemporary church the distinction between evangelist and

40

revivalist are not clearly defined. Further some pastors have a truly prophetic approach in their preaching, such as Johnny Hunt. In fact, Hunt's ministry appears to gather together the three middle leaders: prophet, evangelist, and pastor.

Rather than focusing on lost people outside of the church, the prophet's call is specifically to wake up the people of God from their slumber. His calling matches that of many of the prophets in the Old Testament, who were specifically called to minister to the wandering people of God. The ministry of the revivalist is almost uniquely to the church, while he does not ignore the Great Commission's focus on the lost outside of the church.

Listen for example to the cry of Ezekiel to the chosen people of God:

> "Say to them: '*As* I live,' says the Lord GOD, 'I have no pleasure in the death of the wicked, but that the wicked turn from his way and live. Turn, turn from your evil ways! For why should you die, O house of Israel?'" (Ezek 33:11)

In Ezekiel's quote of God's words to him, we hear the constant cry of God for His own people. This same urgency moved Paul's heart to write his letters to the churches that he had founded. In particular, note the poignant words of Paul to the Galatian churches:

> "I marvel that you are turning away so soon from Him who called you in the grace of Christ, to a different gospel, which is not another; but there are some who trouble you and want to pervert the gospel of Christ. ... O foolish Galatians! Who has bewitched you that you should not obey the truth, before whose eyes Jesus Christ was clearly portrayed among you as crucified?" (Gal 1:6-7; 3:1)

These words of Paul are the words of a prophet-revivalist, calling God's people back to a right relationship with Him.

o **Pioneer Missionaries**

The pioneer missionary is a cross-cultural evangelist. As a "sent one" and apostle, sent by the church and by the Holy Spirit

41

(Acts 13:3-4), the pioneering missionary travels to a pioneer area or another segment of society where the gospel has never been preached and where churches are not yet planted. He may need to learn another language, and he always has to master another cultural identity. Yet God's Holy Spirit has preceded his ministry, wherever he goes, as mentioned in Romans 1:18-25; 2:14-15. For example, J. Hudson Taylor, pioneer missionary to China, expected people to receive Christ the very first time they ever heard of Jesus' name— and some did![3] Today pioneer missionaries are sent to unreached people groups. They are a hybrid of the two leadership gifts, the apostle-evangelist.

   o **Pioneer church planters**

   Church planters are another type of evangelist. The specific role of the pioneer church planter is to evangelize lost people and to nurture them into the fellowship of a local church. They provide a bridge between the work of the evangelist and the role of the pastor. They gather those that they have led to Christ into a small group, and then begin to take on the role of pastor. This was the exact ministry of the Apostle Paul in the Book of Acts. He was an evangelist, a pioneer missionary, a pioneer church planter, and even a pastor (as in Antioch, Acts 11:25-26 and Corinth, Acts 18:8-11). Paul's role also included that of the teacher in Acts 19:9-10. In this case we see how Paul was uniquely qualified to be the example to all Christian leaders in the entire church age (1 Cor 11:1).

---

[3]"The gospel itself is the power of God unto salvation to everyone that believeth. Now, there are different ways of preaching the gospel. There is the plan of preaching the gospel and looking forward to the gradual enlightenment of the people, to their being saved as it were by a process of gradual instruction and preaching. And there is another method of preaching the gospel; *believing it to be the power of God unto salvation;* preaching it in the *expectation* that He who first brought light out of darkness can and will at once and instantaneously take the darkest heathen heart and create light within. That is the method that is successful. It has been my privilege to know many Christians – I am speaking within bounds when I say a hundred – who have accepted Jesus Christ as their Saviour the first time they ever heard of Him. The gospel itself is the power of God unto salvation" (J. Hudson Taylor, "The Source of Power," *Ecumenical Missionary Conference, New York, 1900* [New York, American Tract Society, 1900]: 1:91. emphasis mine).

Some also use special services to plant a church. Such was the case when a Spanish evangelist preached on a side street in Cotonou, Benin. This week of revival meetings led to the a church, the église Baptiste de Menotonin, pastored by Valentin Yehounmey. This revival-to-start-or-restart-a-church methodology has been used effectively for many years. It was used by Evangelist Dr. Robert E. Neighbour (father of Ralph W. Neighbour, Sr.) to restart many closed Baptist churches in New York state in the early 1900s. Later Robbie Roberts, founder of the State Convention of Baptists in Ohio, used the one-week tent revival methodology to found one church after another, leading to the need to found a state convention in 1954. Church planting through revival meetings is effective in rural and urban areas, in the United States and across the globe.

Using this methodology, a church planter teams up with an evangelist, and they target a certain area in need of a local church. They plan a tent revival or some special meetings. With proper preparation and publicity and the gifted preaching of an evangelist, people will respond to the gospel. And, lo and behold, a solid small group of Great Commission believers is gathered as the core of a new church!

These four types of evangelists we have called "biblical types of evangelists." The second main grouping of evangelists we have called "target group evangelists." These evangelists are so named because of their specific ministry or the target group that they reach.

- **Target Group Evangelists**

Two evangelists, known for the target group they reach, are youth evangelists and child evangelists:

o **Youth Evangelists**

Youth are the future, and they need to be reached. A dictum may be, "Youth can best reach youth." Thus, if this saying rings true, it is paramount that young evangelists be raised up, encouraged, and used. Young people bring with them enthusiasm and an

43

understanding of their specific youth culture. They are often full of creative and innovative ideas that only need to be unleashed for the furthering of the gospel among their peers.

Youth evangelists and evangelistic youth bands need to be encouraged and nourished within the local church. Churches should purposefully incorporate youth musicians and youth bands in their various worship events. Adults can very easily crush the creativity and talent of youth by not allowing them to use and polish their gifts within the local church. If the local church does not use their gifts, there are other groups that will be happy to soak up their talents, often in ways that may not glorify the Lord of the harvest.

Youth continue to be a very receptive age group. Fordham noted that Youth Nights are consistently the best attended and most responsive of his revivals. Youth make decisions before their peers and with church youth leaders to moral purity. He encourages them to sign the following commitment card:

"With Jesus in me I will:
"1. Not partake of illegal drugs.
"2. Not partake of alcoholic beverages.
"3. Not participate in pre-marital sex.
"4. Marry an on-fire, Jesus loving Christian, if God ever wants me to marry.
"Signed_____."

Youth flood up to the front of the auditorium or tent to commitment themselves to Jesus in this way. I can think of no better lifestyle commitment for a Christian young person to make.

o **Children Evangelists**

Much children's programming in the local church is geared toward evangelism. It is gospel-focused, and so it should be. God also uses children evangelists to gather this unique and sensitive age group to hear the Gospel. Every church ought to have a child evangelist within its membership, one person whose heart is specially stirred to reach children for Christ. Their gifts should be encouraged and used. Child evangelists also work in multiple church settings, writing curriculum, organizing events, and reaching out to the children beyond the four walls of the church. Some groups have become famous for the emphasis on child evangelism, such as Child Evangelism Fellowship. May God continue to raise up child evangelists.

Along with evangelists that focus directly on a target group, there are also evangelists who have a clear niche in which they function. These require further explanation.

- **More Types of Evangelists**

There also exists several other types of evangelists. These are crusade evangelists, music evangelists, administrative evangelists, and teaching evangelists.

    o **Crusade Evangelists**

The specialization of crusade evangelists differs from that of other preaching evangelists mainly from the size and scope of their meetings. The crusade evangelist often has an appeal that crosses denominational boundaries. This causes the crusade evangelist to wrestle with cooperative strategy and emphasis. Further because the goal is for a larger audience, the venue used tends to necessitate greater resources than a one-church revival. The crusade evangelist, therefore, normally has a significant team working with him. There is the advance team, who works with various groups of pastors and churches to prepare meetings often up to two years in advance. The crusade evangelist generally has a soloist with whom he works and perhaps a choir leader to lead a combined mass choir for the event. All of the needed coordination necessitates a healthy amount of administration. It involves one or more years of full-time work for well-trained individuals to coordinate a major event.

The two complexities in the ministry of the crusade evangelist are: cooperative strategy and funding. Further, there may be a tendency to refrain from preaching the gospel in an unhindered way.

For example as a preaching evangelist in one local church, the evangelist can preach without holding back. However, when faced with multiple denominations working together, combined with the need for funding, the message may be compromised. Much like the issue in missions literature, cooperation focuses on determining the essentials of the gospel. These essentials can be considered anything from the basic Roman Road outline to the eighteen articles of the Baptist Faith and Message (2000). Who is to be invited to join the effort, and who is to be shunned? Cooperation and ecumenism have provided fodder for significant debates for over 150 years of Protestant missionary efforts. May the prospective evangelist avail himself of this large body of literature to learn from the past.

The second complexity to crusade evangelism is the necessity for funding. Large venues require large amounts of money. Some contemporary crusades have cost a significant amount of money not covered by the offerings at the crusades themselves. Thus, fundraisers are needed, and already cash-strapped local churches can find it problematic if they are made to be liable for significant amounts of funding. The crusade evangelist, therefore, needs to balance both cooperation and funding as he plans his evangelistic events. But once these challenges are scaled, crusade evangelism with the right evangelist is probably one of the greatest means to move the Gospel forward in any population or city. In some cases it has resulted in a revival of religion that has reached every level of society and encouraged local churches for years afterward.

- o **Music Evangelists**

Music evangelists provide a wonderful culturally-identified ministry of gospel music to their listeners. In an age when music is so easily available, it is wonderful to have musicians who focus on lifting up the name of Jesus and calling sinners to repent and believe in Jesus Christ.

Some musicians travel with evangelists and sing in their meetings. These musicians allow their talents to be branded with those of the evangelist with whom they travel. Such was the case for Billy Graham who had George Beverly Shea as a soloist and Cliff Barrows to lead mass choirs. Billy Sunday, a crusade evangelist in the early 20th Century, traveled with music evangelist Ira Sankey. J. Wilbur Chapman traveled with musician Charles Alexander. Evangelist Mordecai Ham traveled with his choir director, W. J. Ramsay. In fact, gospel-focused and Jesus-centered music was a hallmark of the revivals of the late 19th and early 20th centuries. The songs that were sung at the meetings continued to nourish the souls and minds of those who heard them long after the tents had been dismantled and the evangelist had moved on to another town. Songs traveled with music evangelists and became imbedded in various hymnals as a result.

Today some contemporary musicians have a strong evangelistic element to their music. They focus on the cross of Jesus, calling sinners to repentance and encouraging God's people to evangelize. These Gospel-centered musicians cross the gamut of musical styles from Country-Gospel to Christian Hip-hop. We need to encourage multiple varieties of musicians. Inspire them to write Bible-filled songs, with a gospel call. Urge them to reach their target group. Recognizing that music is singularly cultural, their music can effectively reach certain segments of society usually unreachable by other styles of music.

o **Administrative Evangelists**

Administrative evangelists organize and lead all different types of evangelism. Burdened by the lack of evangelism among the people of God, this evangelist feels compelled to provide opportunities for God's people to taste and see the Lord at work through direct evangelism. With this burden he organizes and plans evangelism, gradually multiplying the workers. He trains those he goes out with, often with On-the-Job-Training. Victor Benavides is one of these types of evangelists. He is passionate to train and lead out other Christians in street evangelism with Intentional City Evangelism (ICE).

Similarly, the late Presbyterian pastor, D. James Kennedy, developed a reproducible program by which he trained every member of his church desiring training in personal evangelism. The name of this training program was Evangelism Explosion. Its Southern Baptist counterpart was Continuous Witness Training (or C.W.T.). These two programs were phenomenal in training more than a generation of Christians in how to share their faith. The administrative evangelist can also have a far-reaching impact for the gospel.

o   **Teaching Evangelists**

The final evangelist considered under the heading of "more types of evangelists" is the teaching evangelist. This evangelist combines his heart for evangelism with a passion for teaching and study. His setting is the academic climbs of the college and seminary. As is most often the case, he swims against the tide of academia, calling students out of a unique focus on the books and into the streets where lost people are found.

The teaching evangelist must juggle the academic constraints and pressures of publishing and syllabi with motivating and encouraging students to participate in intentional evangelism. Often his students have never been involved in intentional evangelism, nor have they experienced a good example. So the teaching evangelist has a tall task. But he is not alone. Just as all the other evangelists, the most important participant is the Holy Spirit. And because the Holy Spirit speaks and works in, with, and by the Word of God, this evangelist's greatest ally is the Bible rightly interpreted and understood.

A fine example of a teaching evangelist is R. A. Torrey, director of Moody Bible Institute after D. L. Moody passed away in 1899. Torrey combined the erudition of a German-trained mind with a warm heart for lost souls. In so doing, he guided Moody Bible

Institute on a solidly evangelistic path, which remains its heritage to this very day.

Therefore, the teaching evangelist is one of ten evangelists examined in this chapter. All of these are leaders in the church with various cross-hybridization of gifts. They bring an evangelistic spirit to impact everything that they touch. They are the guardians of the Great Commission in Christ's New Testament Church. They also safeguard the doctrine of the church. As a church and denomination honors the worth of its evangelists, so they will all be properly guided by Christ's Great Commission.

CHAPTER FOUR

THE CALL

"What is the point of being an Evangelist if you are not constantly offering people a chance to make things right with God through the Lord Jesus Christ?"

Hyman Appelman

The Lord of the harvest is still calling out across time, requesting those with ears to hear to also have a heart to respond. "Whom shall I send, and who will go for Us?" It is our conviction in writing this book that Christ is not only calling, but He has also gifted and prepared evangelists for the harvest fields at home and abroad. Nor does it appear that the problem with the harvest is on God's end. He is still Lord of the harvest, and He is still calling out. He is still gifting, preparing, and calling. The problem seems to be on our end. That is on the human side of the equation. Are we taking the time to listen to His voice, really listen? Are we willing, really willing? Willing to run to obey His voice?

Just like a footrace on earth, a roadmap is always helpful. This chapter will discuss the question, how can you know if you are called to the ministry of evangelist? And if so, what are some concrete steps that you can take to fulfill your ministry and calling.

Testing God's Call for Our Lives

1. Listen to the Yearning in Your Heart:

Consider for example God's calling in the heart of a certain Levite in the Old Testament:

- Deut 8:6-8, "So if a Levite comes from any of your gates, from where he dwells among all Israel, and comes with all the desire of his mind to the place which the LORD chooses, then he may serve in the name of the LORD his God as all his brethren the Levites *do*, who stand there before the LORD. They shall have equal portions to eat, besides what comes from the sale of his inheritance."

Here, in God's Word, we have the example of God leading a person to serve Him by placing a desire in his mind. This particular Levite had a yearning in his heart to serve the Lord in what would ultimately become Jerusalem, that is, in the place God chose to place His Name. And this yearning became so strong within him, that he left his home and traveled to Jerusalem to set himself at the disposal of the Levites there. God made a way, in His word, for this Levite to minister and to be provided for, as he followed the yearning of his heart.

Psalm 37:4 also parallels this thought, "Delight yourself also in the LORD, And He shall give you the desires of your heart." God begins to shape the desires of our heart as we delight in Him and in His word. As we do so, He places in us a desire to serve Him.

Often this godly desire will be fueled by several things:

- First, by seeing an example of an evangelist or preacher sold out to Jesus.
- Second, by listening as the Word of God is preached, and the flame of the Holy Spirit placing a desire to serve Him in your heart.
- Third, by being invited by the preacher to share with the congregation the urging of the Spirit in your heart.

We will later see the importance of the affirmation of God's people on His hand in your life.

So the first stage in understanding the call of God upon your life is to essay your own heart. Next, you need to start seeking opportunities to serve. These opportunities will be the testing ground in which you will begin to understand and hone the gift set that God has given you, in order to understand how God wants to use your life to His glory.

2. Take Action in Opportunities that God Places Before You:

Along with the urgings that God gives in man's heart, God also gives opportunities to serve him. It is important that the man of God who is seeking the will of God avail himself of the opportunities to serve that God provides. Jesus said:

- Luke 16:10, "He who *is* faithful in *what is* least is faithful also in much; and he who is unjust in *what is* least is unjust also in much."

So also, if a man feels called of the Lord, he should seek out opportunities to serve Him, no matter how small they may appear to be. Every soul matters to the Lord, no matter how poor or how disconnected to society.

If you feel called to evangelism, it is imperative that you seek out opportunities to evangelize wherever and whenever you can find them. The local church is a great place to serve. Go forward when the pastor or evangelist gives an invitation. Let the church know what the Lord is doing in your heart. Perhaps the pastor will give you an opportunity to preach or to minister in some way.

Right away, you need to be a self-starter and begin to learn the basics of evangelism. Try to find someone who loves souls, ask them for help. The basics or personal evangelism include:

- Memorizing a Gospel plan;
- Learning to engage a lost soul in conversation about Christ;
- Knowing how to lead a person prepared by the Holy Spirit to pray to receive Christ as their Savior;
- Making evangelism a regular part of your life.

The basics of preaching evangelism also include:

- Preaching a Gospel message;
- Giving a clear invitation to receive salvation in Christ.

If you cannot find anyone who can help you learn these things, then you need to look for someone. It may be an evangelist, a youth pastor, a senior pastor, a deacon, a professor of evangelism, or a college campus minister. Pray for God to place someone like this on your path, and do not give up praying and seeking until He answers that prayer. This is where mentoring, on the job training, and opportunities to preach are vitally important. Read the autobiographies of evangelists. A good book on evangelism is also helpful, but it is best to link up with a person who can guide you.

As you are learning to share your faith, be faithful in availing yourself of daily opportunities that God brings your way. It may very well be that He will give you such a burden that your heart will almost pound out of your chest. You may begin to cry because of the great need, and the impossibility of you, one person, to ever meet the crying need. The word of God will also fuel your soul developing a burden. Verses in the Bible may jump out at you. Write them down and memorize them. Let them sink deeply in your soul.

Here are some verses that have been extremely motivating for us evangelistically:

- Ezek 3:18-19, "When I say to the wicked, 'You shall surely die,' and you give him no warning, nor speak to warn the wicked from his wicked way, to save his life, that same wicked *man* shall die in his iniquity; but his blood I will require at your hand. Yet, if you warn the wicked, and he does not turn from his wickedness, nor from his wicked way, he shall die in his iniquity; but you have delivered your soul."
- Acts 17:16-17, "Now while Paul waited for them at Athens, his spirit was provoked within him when he saw that the city was given over to idols. Therefore he reasoned in the synagogue with the Jews and with the *Gentile* worshipers, and in the marketplace daily with those who happened to be there."

- 1 Cor 1:17 (our revision), "For Christ did not send me to baptize, but to evangelize, not with wisdom of words, lest the cross of Christ should be made of no effect."
- 1 Cor 9:16-17 (our revision), "For if I evangelize, I have nothing to boast of, for necessity is laid upon me; yes, woe is me if I do not evangelize! For if I do this willingly, I have a reward; but if against my will, I have been entrusted with a stewardship."

Please let the verses God lays on your heart, as you read or handwrite Scripture, resound in your mind. You will best accomplish this goal by memorizing and reciting them.

As your mind and heart are being shaped and stamped by the Word of God, it is almost a fact that He will begin to give you a vision to do things that you are not now doing. You will see lost souls in a new way. Your burden will be so great that you will want to do something. Praise the Lord! This is the Holy Spirit working in you. Ask God to guide you into developing new evangelistic outreaches, new Gospel plans, new evangelistic services, new Gospel music, and/or new evangelism teams. Serve as a counselor in your home church and in other church revivals in your area. The list is endless.

3. Make Opportunities to Share the Gospel:

This is where the evangelist has served the church throughout its centuries. Evangelists have been at the forefront of new ministries, new schools, and new organizations from time immemorial. Even before you go to school to get further education, start something new. Begin a new ministry at your church, under the leadership of your pastor. Preach every opportunity you get. Begin a new Bible study at your college or university. Start a new prayer group, start an evangelism team; do something!

If you want to taste and see that the Lord is good, you need to put Him to the test. He has taught you His Word, now it is up to you to, based on the promises of His Word, begin to go for it. Start practicing what you are learning. It is not without reason that God's Word has this following admonition:

- Eccl 11:9, "Rejoice, O young man, in your youth, And let your heart cheer you in the days of your youth; Walk in the ways of your heart, And in the sight of your eyes; But know that for all these God will bring you into judgment."

Consider also:

- Isa 54:2, "Enlarge the place of your tent, And let them stretch out the curtains of your dwellings; Do not spare; Lengthen your cords, And strengthen your stakes."

Or consider:

- Joel 2:28-29, "And it shall come to pass afterward That I will pour out My Spirit on all flesh; Your sons and your daughters shall prophesy, Your old men shall dream dreams, Your young men shall see visions. And also on *My* menservants and on *My* maidservants I will pour out My Spirit in those days."

Don't be discouraged if opportunities to evangelize are not given to you. You need to make them happen. Tap into the youthful vigor that God has given you by His Holy Spirit and begin to dream dreams. Start moving. When Tom was in college, the late Steve Ross told him in a Bible study, "You can't steer a parked car." So get moving, no matter what, and God can steer you in His direction.

Several sayings that come to mind at this point:

- William Carey, pioneer missionary of the Great Century of Protestant missions, said, "Expect great things from God; attempt great things for God."
- In 1967 D. L. Moody was challenged by Henry Varley, "The world has yet to see what God can do with one man wholly committed to Him." Moody's response was, "I will be that man!" Moody was 30 years old. He died 32 years later in 1899. Praise the Lord for what He did through this evangelist.
- Or consider a saying sometimes attributed to Dixon Host, director of the China Inland Mission after Hudson Taylor died, "If you

want to get something done, give it to young men, they will get it done."

Fordham confirms the need for a zeal, endurance, and an aggressive spirit to fulfill the calling of the evangelist:

"Over the years I have noticed that the men, who are willing to send out fliers, meet with pastors, and do whatever it takes to go fulltime have been the ones who are fulltime. They take any meeting that comes along in their early days, and will even go to places where they know it will cost them financially to go, because the Spirit of God has made the call as an evangelist so abundantly clear. This burning fire that the Holy Spirit has placed in them allows them to continue against all criticism and hindrance from friends, family, and others.

"Because 98% of men who enter the work every year drop out, the Spirit of God's clear call is a must. Read the lives of evangelists of today and those who have gone on before. See where their lives coincide with yours. Mordecai Ham's 'call was a continual and irresistible urge' which he resisted for some time. God used his circumstances and his family to influence him in a great way. He yielded to God, borrowed $1,700 moved in with his in-laws, and began to study. His first sermon he was told to preach on the spur of the moment. He was asked to preach at a revival, and the people responded and several were saved. The pastor got angry at Mordecai because the people came forward when Mordecai preached, but would not come when he preached. This pastor had no understanding of the office of the evangelist. In time doors began to open, and Ham's ministry took off.[1] Most evangelists have a slow difficult start, but not all."[2]

By the way, Mordecai Ham was the evangelist God used to bring a young man named Billy Graham to Christ in Charlotte, N.C. in 1934. Graham followed Ham's approach in tent revivals in his early ministry of evangelism.

Because opportunities to evangelize are not always easily found, make opportunities. Attempt little things; attempt great things. Lost

---

[1] Edward E. Ham, *Fifty Years On The Battlefront With Christ: A Biography Of Mordecai F. Ham* (Nashville: Hermitage for the Old Kentucky Home Revivalist, n.d.).
[2] Fordham, unpublished manuscript.

people are everywhere. Begin from the outset to make the fulfilling of the Great Commission your highest goal and priority.

4. Value the Input from Godly People:

As you begin to minister the Gospel, God's people will take notice. It is very important that you stay positive in regards to your local church, and seek their affirmation and encouragement. It is at this point that zealous young men can begin to judge their local church and begin to find fault with it. This is a great danger that needs to be avoided. Stay sweet. Remember what Jesus said:

- Matt 7:1-2, "Judge not, that you be not judged. For with what judgment you judge, you will be judged; and with the measure you use, it will be measured back to you."

Although it may not appear to be the case, there are others in the church who have been moved by the Holy Spirit just as you are. They will understand and will affirm you. You need their encouragement and support in the future. To be real candid, you need their support if you feel called to go for further training in seminary. You will need a letter of endorsement from your pastor. You may also need their financial support if God calls you to be a full-time vocational evangelist. Now is not the time to get conceited about how God is using you. In fact, it is never the time to get conceited!

Further, at this stage it will be important to listen to the counsel of some godly saints who know you. They will help you by giving ideas for you to improve your ministry and ideas for further training. Young Moses needed to be open to the counsel of his father-in-law, Jethro, who saw that he was burning himself out. Moses was doing the right thing, but he was doing it inefficiently. It was not good for Moses, nor for his family, nor for those to whom he was ministering:

- Exod 18:17-23, "So Moses' father-in-law said to him, 'The thing that you do *is* not good. Both you and these people who *are* with you will surely wear yourselves out. For this thing *is* too much for you; you are not able to perform it by yourself. Listen now to my voice; I will give you counsel, and God will be with you: Stand before God for the people, so that you may bring the difficulties to God. And you shall teach them the statutes and the laws, and show them the way in which they must walk and the work they must do. Moreover you shall select from all the people able men, such as fear God, men of truth, hating covetousness; and place *such* over them *to be* rulers of thousands, rulers of hundreds, rulers of fifties, and rulers of tens. And let them judge the people at all times. Then it will be *that* every great matter they shall bring to you, but every small matter they themselves shall judge. So it will be easier for you, for they will bear *the burden* with you. If you do this thing, and God *so* commands you, then you will be able to endure, and all this people will also go to their place in peace.'"

Fortunately, Moses was open and sensitive to the advice of his father-in-law. And it was better for him and for those to whom he was ministering. Similarly, God will bring into your path people who will act like Jethros. They will give you advice and good ideas. Yes, there may be someone like the old prophet who misled the young man of God from Judah who prophesied against King Jeroboam's altar in Bethel (see 1 Kings 13). So great wisdom is needed here. It is no wonder that before Jesus sent out His disciples, he gave them a solemn warning:

- Matt 10:16, "Behold, I send you out as sheep in the midst of wolves. Therefore be wise as serpents and harmless as doves."

Remember that Jesus too ministered as a traveling evangelist:

- Mark 1:37-38, "When they found Him, they said to Him, 'Everyone is looking for You.' But He said to them, 'Let us go into the next towns, that I may preach there also, because for this purpose I have come forth.'"
- Luke 4:42-43 (our revision), "Now when it was day, He departed and went into a deserted place. And the crowd sought Him and came to Him, and tried to keep Him from leaving them; but He said to them, 'I must evangelize the kingdom of God to the other cities also, because for this purpose I have been sent.'"

Jesus faced the same antagonism that you will face. He faced the same hostile crowds (and worse), as well as the same open individuals. The Apostle Paul also faced both good times and very bad times. The Bible, its examples and teachings, will become like sweet oil to your soul as you begin to experience the reproach of the Gospel.

5. Ask God to Direct You as to His Specific Call on Your Life:

How are you to know the specific call that God has for you? Jeremiah was set aside before he was formed in his mother's womb. He was called to be a prophet before he was born:

- Jer 1:4-5, "Then the word of the LORD came to me, saying, 'Before I formed you in the womb I knew you; Before you were born I sanctified you; I ordained you a prophet to the nations.'"

Not only are we called to salvation before the foundations of the earth (Eph 1:3-5), but all our days are written in a book (Psa 139:16). Yes, God knows and cares about the calling that He has on your life. And the calling of a New Testament evangelist is not easy, just like the call of the Old Testament prophet was not easy. But even in pain or prison, the prophets, apostles, and evangelists were in God's perfect plan.

One reason for the numerous types of evangelists listed in Chapter Three is to open your eyes as to how God has used and called evangelists in the past. Being an evangelist is not a monolithic idea. There is variety and variation in how God calls and uses His people. Therefore, use Chapter Three as a mirror to see in what ways God has gifted you and fitted you for His ministry. God has a will for you. And He will guide you in that will. He will not leave you nor forsake you. He will do it:

- Psa 32:8, "I will instruct you and teach you in the way you should go; I will guide you with My eye."

Here are five concrete questions from Stephen Olford that you should ask, as you seek to discern whether God is calling you as an evangelist:

1. Do I meet the qualifications of an evangelist, as set forth in the Word of God (Acts 6:3)?
2. Is there the witness of the Spirit in my heart that God has called me?
3. Has the gift of the evangelist become evident in my life and service?
4. Has my church recognized and confirmed my evangelistic gift?
5. Has God been pleased to use my evangelistic gift of the salvation souls?[3]

Amen! As a leader in the church, the evangelist should follow the same list of qualifications as found in 1 Tim 3. He should have a sense of calling in his life. God's gifting should be evident by his life and service. People in his local church should see and affirm that gift. And God will confirm the gift by allowing the evangelist to harvest souls for His kingdom.

If you are unsure of your calling as an evangelist, but you are sensing the leading of the Lord in this area, keep this book open to the list above, and prayerfully read through each of the five questions given to us by Stephen Olford. Ask God for a confirmation of each one of these points, one by one. God will make clear to you His will. You may want to write the date when each one of these is confirmed in the margin, as an encouragement to you in the future, when you will certainly face days of doubt, discouragement, or despondency.

If you lack confirmation in any of these areas, you may not be called to be an evangelist. Even so, God has wonderful work in His harvest for you. If you are called to be a pastor, God's word still says, "Do the work of an evangelist" (2 Tim 4:5). Value evangelists, use evangelists, imitate evangelists, and prepare for the coming of the evangelist!

---

[3]Adapted from Stephen Olford, "The Evangelist's Gift and Ministry," in *The Work of an Evangelist*, edited by J. D. Douglas (Minneapolis: World Wide, 1984), 143-45.

Two Examples of God's Calling Evangelists

Evangelist J. Harold Smith:

"But even with all this emphasis on church, I was not 'born again.' I had joined the church and been baptized when I was twelve because I noticed my mother tended to dab at her eyes during the invitation time in our church services. My friends were joining up, so I made everyone happy by going forward and presenting myself as a candidate for baptism one Sunday morning.

"The next week I was baptized, but when I tried to pull off my wet pants, jumping up and down on one foot, I produced a chorus of oaths that took the starch right out of the deacon's collar. The only change involved in that experience involved changing nothing more than my clothes.

"Since I was now a bona-fide member of the church in good standing, I really didn't think much about what it meant to be really saved. There weren't any radio or television preachers around talking about it, either. I became more and more saddened, and disillusioned, and desperate.

"Then on September 4, 1932, while sitting with my sister, Mildred, on her front porch in Greenville, South Carolina, she looked me squarely in the face and said, 'You have tried everything that the Devil has to offer. Why don't you give Jesus Christ a chance in your heart?' I turned to rebuke her, but the Holy Spirit gripped my heart and for the first time in my life I really prayed, calling upon the Lord and asking Him to cleanse my soul from all of my sins.

"I think my exact words were, 'God have mercy on me a sinner. Save me through Jesus Christ.' And that's when I was really born again. I became a child of God and just as I knew that at that moment my name was written in the Lamb's Book of Life for all eternity. I knew that I was going to give my life to the preaching of the Gospel.

"Sometimes we experience a 'knowing' that is so sure and so powerful for us, that by comparison, tables and chairs and food, and light and, dark seem unreal. I really knew about my salvation and my calling, and I have never doubted either since that moment. ...

"I believe that the heaviest temptation of my life came in the next few hours on that same day. I felt my heart start to beat faster as I realized I had to go face that girl I met eleven years ago in that grocery store and tell her I had been saved... and was going to be a preacher, not a medical doctor.

"The Devil was real to me that evening. I had never had but one sweetheart. I never loved any girl but her. And the Devil said to me, 'She's going to drop you, old buddy. She's too classy a dame to marry a preacher.'

"But I knew I had to tell her; the sooner the better.

"She was working at the Greenville News, and I went by to pick her up. She knew something was going on when she got in the car, but I waited until I was inside her living room to tell her. I said straight-out, 'You'd better sit down. I have something to tell you. I'm going to be a preacher. I was saved this afternoon.'

"And she was silent for what seemed like light years. Time is such a strange phenomenon. When we're happy and busy, it seems to fly; at other times it drags. During that little slice of time, during her silence— I lived and died a thousand lifetimes; it was long enough for whole continents to rise and sink; it was so prolonged a silence, I could have filled it with all of man's recorded history, re-writ; it was so lengthy, I circled the globe twelve times on a tricycle.

"But when she spoke, she simply said, 'Harold, ever since I was twelve years old, I have wanted to marry a Baptist preacher.' Those were words worth waiting for. And so, thirteen months later, we were married." [4]

Evangelist Charles Finney:

"His call and conversion were simultaneous. He met Christ and was gloriously saved. The morning after he was saved a client came into his office and asked him if he were ready to try his case which was set for 10 o'clock that day. Finney replied, 'I have a retainer from the Lord Jesus Christ to plead His cause and I cannot plead your cause.' 'When the client left,' said Finney, 'I immediately went forth to talk to those I would meet about their souls. I knew that God wanted me to preach the Gospel, and that I must begin immediately. I knew it with a certainty beyond all possibility of a doubt!'"[5]

---

[4]J. Harold Smith, *The Time of My Life: The Autobiography of J. Harold Smith* (Orlando: Daniels, 1981), 22-24.

[5]Walter Knight, *Treasury of Illustrations* (Grand Rapids: Eerdmans, 1967), 287-88.

CHAPTER FIVE

GETTING STARTED

"Receiving a call to be an itinerant evangelist is one of the greatest joys I can imagine. It is also one of the most difficult tasks in the body of Christ."

Rick Barton

Along with the call to the ministry of the evangelist, getting started is one of the biggest road blocks to "doing the work of an evangelist." While the exact order of events and the leading of the Lord differs with each man, this chapter will enumerate some important aspects for getting started in the work of the evangelist.

1. The Effective Evangelist Must Be Thoroughly Saved

Because the call to the ministry of the evangelist is closely tied to one's assurance of salvation, evangelists have often had very dramatic conversions. The power of their conversion provides them the grit that they need to continue in the ministry when it becomes difficult. Their conversion gives them the assurance that the message of the Gospel is absolutely the most important message in life! Their salvation may be as unusual and exciting as Paul's meeting with Christ on the Damascus Road or as plain as a young boy asking for forgiveness. The admonition of Paul stands as a stark reminder: "But you must continue in the things which you have learned and been assured of" (2 Tim 3:14).

An evangelist shared his conversion story:

"In 1958, a motorcycle policeman in Atlanta, Georgia caught three eight-year-old boys. One had thrown a rock over a tractor-trailer and hit a 1959 Ford windshield. The windshield cracked and the driver rounded up a police officer. He came back down Interstate 75 southbound in the right lane. The motorcycle policeman was in the left lane hiding behind the 1959 Ford until he spotted the boys. The three were quickly apprehended. The police called their parents. Each boy blamed the other two. When one of the boys got home, his father normally would have taken off his belt and whipped the boy. Instead of whipping him, he told the boy he was too disappointed in him to whip him. The young man was so crushed by his guilt that he began to try to be a good boy. He began to make A's in school. He batted .600 in little league. At night during the summer he would often get in the back of a pick-up truck and pray that someone would tell him how to be saved. No one came; no Sunday School teacher or preacher came to explain the simple plan of salvation. His family moved during the following year. The boy began to go to Sunday School, Christian Training, and R.A's with the next-door neighbors. Every Sunday morning the Sunday School teacher told his class just before the closing prayer, 'Boys, Jesus Christ died on the cross for your sins. If you would ask Him, He will forgive your sins.' The boy heard, but he did not understand. A few months later, the boys' class got out of Christian Training before the adults. The boys began to hit each other on the arm to see who could hit the hardest. One of the older boys, Tommy Neal, came over to this young man and said, 'Keith, Jesus Christ died on the cross for your sins.' The boy answered, 'I know it'—he had really heard that before in Sunday School. Tommy said, 'If you'd ask Jesus to save you, He would save you right now!' The boy answered, 'I would like to, but I don't know what to say to Jesus.' Tommy said, 'Let's get on our knees and I will help you with the words. Just say, "Lord Jesus, please come into my heart and forgive my sins."' The boy did just that, and Jesus Christ came into his heart and forgave every sin. At the evening Revival service, Evangelist Ed Vallowe preached and gave the invitation. He said a prayer and the congregation began to sing, 'Have Thine Own Way.' Before the congregation got the H sound out on *Have*, the first word of the first verse, The boy ran down the aisle and told the pastor, Dr. Paul Gilliam, that Christ had saved him and that he was ready to do whatever God said next. That boy could hardly wait to go home to tell his parents. He went to school the next day and told his teacher and all of his friends. He felt that if people just knew that Christ died for them, then they could have the joy, which he knew in Christ. In fact that young man now has a lifelong desire to do nothing, but tell men how to be saved. That boy became an evangelist and is now coauthoring this book."

Every evangelist must have a dramatic conversion to Christ or at the very least a clear sense of what salvation means. That does not mean that the evangelist has to be saved from a life of alcoholism, drug addiction, or sexual perversion to be an effective evangelist. But it does mean that he needs to have a clear-cut salvation experience. That conversion must include a deep conviction of sin by God's Holy Spirit. It should include a God-given drive to tell everyone about Christ. While it is true that some evangelists lived in great immorality prior to coming to Christ, any sin will bring a man to hell. A testimony of salvation that holds back a young man even from sipping a beer is a powerful testimony in these times of debauchery. The same type of backbone is needed to persuasively present Christ.

2. The Effective Evangelist Must Have a Clear Call

While we noted five important steps to discerning God's call in Chapter Four, it must be lived out in the life of the one who is called. This call often leads to a wrestling match with God, as God brings His servants into complete submission to His will.

Keith continued his testimony:

"After I was saved I lived red-hot for Jesus for the next two years. But in the seventh grade, I got too big for my britches and was puffed up with pride. I was on a championship football team. I was not putting Christ first in my life.

"That summer I went to Camp Joy just out of Chattanooga, Tennessee. I knew that if any camper needed to rededicate his life it was I. I went forward on Thursday night and told Dr. Buffington I was saved and just needed to get right with God. He had prayer with me and told me to talk with my counselor back in the cabin. My turn to talk came just after midnight. As we shared I began to realize that not only did I need to recommit my life to Christ, but also that God was calling me for full-time Christian service. I wrote on a blank page in the back of my Bible that God had called me to fulltime service on that date in 1963.

"When I got home for eighth grade, football started and the banquets started. I told the Lord I would go to church Sunday morning, Sunday Night, Wednesday night, and go out on visitation on Thursdays. But I would not be fulltime for Him. I tore the page out of the back of my Bible on which I had written my commitment to ministry. I wadded it up and threw it in the trashcan. I was as active in church as anyone you have ever seen, and yet I was a million miles out of the will of God.

"The next fall I had mononucleosis. I missed most of the football season and had a relapse when I went out for track. My tenth grade year my thighbone was broken. I was in the South Fulton Hospital in a body cast Saturday night after surgery. Deacons had to go out of the room so the football coach could come in. He said, 'I knew you were a Christian, I just did not realize how active you were in church.' The deacons chimed in saying that I was the kind of boy I ought to be. But my pastor did not say a word. He caught me alone on Sunday afternoon and told me the reason I was in a body cast—and not only a short cast either, but one from my chest down to my foot. I was running from God. My pastor said, 'God will keep you flat of your back, 'till you get right with Him.' I knew he was right. I thought he was the only one who knew that God was calling me to fulltime service.

"I fought that call until the first Saturday in December 1967. On that morning I told my mom and dad God was calling me. On Sunday morning at the age of seventeen, I went forward and took Dr. F. J. Hendrix, interim pastor, by the hand. I told him that God was calling me for fulltime service. He said that God had called me to preach and he knew it the first time he saw me. I replied that I did not know if it was to preach. But I was willing to dig ditches, crawl through the sewers of Atlanta, be a missionary in Africa, or to do whatever God wanted me to do. He said, 'God has called you to preach and we are going to license you today.' The church backed me in God's calling and I was licensed that day.

"I preached my first sermon in January 1968. It was pathetic. I did such a poor job, I told the Lord I would never preach again. God intervened and I was called to preach a youth night at First Baptist Mountain View, Georgia. I told the Lord I would preach if He gave me a sermon. He did and heaven came down. I preached my first revival at my home church that summer and now over 1,500 revivals and harvest days later I am still going."

While some might consider this example of the call of God a case of emotional enthusiasm, several questions should be considered:

- If God does not call by moving upon the emotions of a person, then how does He call someone to ministry for Him? Is there another way?
- Did not this call stick, in the example of Keith Fordham? It lasted him over 44 years of grueling evangelism ministry!

To the discerning heart, it will be made clear that God must move our will even as He moves our rational being. And God must move the will of the prospective evangelist to be completely dead to self, to worldly ambition, and to selfish gain, and to count himself alive all and only for the Gospel. Now that is quite an overhaul that God must accomplish in our lives!

One thing is certain; a man will not stay in the work of the evangelist if he does not know that God has called him. In the financial difficulties of the first two years, 98% of men move out of evangelism and go into the pastorate or some other work. The certainty that God has called a man to be an evangelist will force him to stay on his knees until God shows him the way.

3. The Effective Evangelist Must Publicize

John Bisagno said that if God gives a man to His church as an evangelist that he will be confirmed and affirmed by his brethren. Bisagno was correct, however, there may be some time span between a man knowing God's call in his heart, and the affirmation and confirmation by pastors of local churches. The reason for this is that pastors of churches may not know that a particular evangelist exists. Consequently, the very first step a man must take on entering evangelism, is to mail or put out publicity. Again, with a clear call, the evangelist will consequently feel unashamed to publicize his availability for meetings.

In 1975, the Home Mission Board (now NAMB) of the Southern Baptist Convention recommended that vocational evangelists mail out at least 6,000 brochures twice a year to churches running two hundred or more in Sunday School. This brochure was to include some biographical information and pastoral recommendations, especially important in the early years of an evangelist's ministry. Further, it is important to remember that the evangelist's photo be on the front of the brochure, with his name in large, bold letters.

Some Quick Ideas for Effective Brochures

- Make it colorful
- Photo of evangelist on the front cover, as well as his name in bold
- Be sure to include pertinent contact information on the back cover
- Include experience you have had and quotes of pastors who can be references to your ministry
- Include ministry emphases (children, VBS, youth, music, artwork, etc.), special talents (playing the trumpet, drama, humor, etc.), with photos of the same
- Consider adding special sermon series that you have prepared
- Don't overload it with too much small print; make it readable with some blank spaces
- Look into the process of third class mailing before you send them out (there is a process of getting enrolled for third class mail).

Now some may object to using human means of publicity for spiritual work. The Bible says of salvation, "And how shall they hear without a preacher?" (Rom 10:14) The same applies to the ministry of the evangelist. How will pastors hear of his ministry, unless someone tells them. A good brochure, website, and/or blog can be very effective to that end.

Further, while hard copy mailings are still important, which is clear from the junk mail that we receive every day, if done properly emails can also be effective in communicating about the ministry of an evangelist. It is also recommended that the email should have an imbedded link to a website where a form can be filled out for further information on the evangelist's availability.

Some Ideas for Effective Websites

- Have a theme design for your website
- Put your name and photo on the home page
- Include a page that gives your biography
- Include a page with some sample sermons in audio or video formats
- Include your brochure online, or something like it
- Check the websites of other evangelists, to see how they are organized and what kind of material that they include, see:
  - Keith Fordham's www.keithfordham.com;
  - Junior Hill's www.juniorhillministries.com; and
  - Bill Britt's www.compelministries.org.

As these means of communication are used, pray for God's blessing over the communication being sent out, before it is sent out. Keith seeks God's leading as he has sends out brochures to pastors that he does not know:

> "It has been my experience from the first mailing of brochures until this one in year thirty-eight of evangelism, that a minimum of five to twelve men call and say, 'I was in my office praying when I received your brochure, and God told me to call you. Even though I do not know you or anyone who recommended you, I was impressed by God to have you in for a revival meeting.'"

Nuts and Bolts of Getting Started

Keith gave a testimony of his start in the work of the evangelist:

> "Upon finishing New Orleans Seminary in January 1975, I moved to Atlanta. God touched a pastor to give me some advice. That pastor sat down with me and told me to go to as many evangelism conferences

as possible so that I could meet pastors and hand out my brochures. The Florida, Georgia, Alabama, and South Carolina Evangelism Conferences proved to be fruitful places for making the necessary contacts with pastors.

"Among the first men I went to see was an Associational Missionary to seek advice on entering vocational Evangelism. He said there is no such thing as the office of the evangelist. That office had ended with the passing of the Apostles in the first century. I just went on to another missionary who believed the Bible.

"God put it on this next man's heart to print 6,000 brochures for me. The only cost, which I had to pay, was the cost of the paper. God knew that I had very little money to spend in printing up a brochure. That missionary's name was Harold Graham. God also knew that I needed the opportunity to work at what He had called me to do. That same missionary personally encouraged six pastors in his association to use me that first year. Without the help and encouragement of that dear associational missionary, I might have not survived that first year in evangelism.

"In 1975, Bobby Sunderland of the Home Mission Board said that if a man had at least twelve revivals in his first year in evangelism, then he should stay in the work for a second year. I would like to add to that statement that he should have at least twenty to twenty-five meetings the second year, and he should have more than thirty meetings per year thereafter. This number of meetings is a confirmation of God's gifting as an evangelist. If the pattern of twelve meetings does not grow to thirty meetings or more in a year, it is a good indication that a man needs to consider something besides being an itinerant, revival evangelist.

"In my first year, I held 17 meetings. In the second year, I had 26 revivals, and I have had anywhere from 30 to 43 revival meetings every year thereafter, not including Bible studies, retreats, and camps."

Another venue for publicity is state papers. We strongly recommend that the young evangelist purchase ads in several nearby state papers. Your picture, the fact you are an evangelist, how to contact you and find your website should all be placed in the ad.

Your phone numbers, office and/or cell phone, and your home phone should be listed. Your e-mail address should be prominent as well.

4. Take Every Opportunity That Comes Your Way

At the beginning, the opportunity to preach in the county seat churches will not likely be there. That's okay. Take every opportunity that you can, with the needs of your wife and family in mind, if that is your situation. The ministry of the evangelist is a spiritual one. The Holy Spirit guided Philip both to preach in the city of Samaria, as well as go to the desert road to speak with one man. While finances will likely be very tight, it is important from the outset that finances do not drive your ministry. The Holy Spirit should drive your ministry! Be careful of getting dollar signs in your eyes early in your ministry. That was not the example of Jesus.

5. Start Something

In the history of the church, evangelists are God's entrepreneurs given to the church. Evangelists have started schools. In fact, most of the prominent colleges in the United States were founded by evangelists and those with hearts for conversion: Basil Manly founded Furman University; Gilbert Tennent founded what became Princeton University; Eleazar Wheelock founded Dartmouth University; and so forth. Evangelists have founded orphanages, rescue missions, and foreign mission boards. Most lasting evangelistic agencies in Protestant, Evangelical, and Baptist churches were started by evangelists. In fact, it appears that God has chosen the evangelist to be the innovator in his church, as he leads the charge to fulfill the Great Commission.

How does that apply to your call?

- Evangelist, consider founding a not-for-profit for your own support and ministry;
- Evangelist, consider founding schools, orphanages, and rescue missions;

- Evangelist, found tract societies, Bible societies, and other literature societies;
- Music evangelist, write gospel-centered songs and publish them, publish hymn books and song books;
- Evangelist, plant churches, revitalize dead churches, grow existing churches.

The ministry of the evangelist must be unleashed. He is vital to the leadership of the Christ's church. In fact, without the work of an evangelist, it may be questioned whether any church is truly Christ's church at all!

Pros and Cons of Starting a Not-For-Profit Organization:

Two testimonies: First, Keith Fordham's:

"Seventeen revivals are not enough to make a living financially in a beginning year of vocational evangelism. In 1975, I received approximately $7,000 in church offerings and nearly $6,000 in individual gifts. Without the existence of the Keith Fordham Evangelistic Association, Inc., I would never have made it through the first years of evangelism, nor could the ministry have been as effective as it has been."

Second, Tom Johnston's:

"This chapter has been convicting for me, because when I was young I thought that I was too spiritual to ask anyone for financial help. Yes, I started a Not-For-Profit in 1985 called Evangelism Unlimited, Inc. But it was not until 1995 that I first considered requesting that proceeds from Evangelism Unlimited assist me in supporting my family. That meant that for 10 years I had to look for other full-time or part-time jobs to support my growing family.

"Hindsight being 20:20, had I had the advice in this book early on, the Lord may have led my life to be more completely devoted to preaching evangelism and soul-winning. Please young evangelist, don't be stubborn like me, but listen to the good advice of those that have gone before you."

There are at least two types of organizations. Both have strengths and weaknesses. The first is "no organization," and the second is an evangelistic association. What is meant by "no organization?" It means that the evangelist has only his personal bank account. He is paid after all expenses are met from all the church offerings that are received. He has no organized prayer chain. He has feasting one week and famine the next. He has no financial base to supplement the church love offerings.

The strengths of "no organization" are abundant:

- There is no annual CPA audit of an association, and the fees that go with it;
- A timely offering can be used to pay off debts;
- Office expense is less;
- A man who launches out of a successful pastorate may have more than thirty revivals his first year and may have an even higher salary than he did as pastor—the reason for this is that the love offerings establish his salary;
- There are fewer tax forms to file.

The weaknesses of "no organization" are also manifold:

- A man may be tempted to mishandle his money;[1]
- Because he is not accountable to anyone, he may be accused of mishandling funds;
- He cannot make future plans for ministry as easily with no base of support (travel expenses, printing costs, publishing books, web development costs, etc.);
- He will tend to be less organized and prepared;
- He will be less likely to incur prayer support;
- He can give no tax-exempt credit for gifts received from individuals, unless it is done through a church.[2]

---

[1]For instance, might spend his money during times of revival (March through the first three weeks of May; the second week of July up through the week before Labor Day weekend; and the second week of September through the week before Thanksgiving), and not be able to provide for his family's needs from Thanksgiving through February, and also for the month of June.

One example of this last difficulty occurred in a Georgia church. The evangelist had an annual banquet; pledges were made to the evangelist during this January meeting. Since he was out of funds and the pledges were given directly to the local church, the evangelist drew funds out of the church's account on the pledges that had been made, but which had not yet been given. Needless to say, a mild furor ensued. The difficulty was ironed out when the church placed these funds in a separate special bank account. Consequently, funds could not be drawn out if they did not yet exist, and no strain was placed on the church budget.

The second approach is that of founding a Not-For-Profit evangelistic organization. Likewise, there are at least two types of these organizations. One type has a large board of directors while the second type has a small board of trusted friends as directors.

The large board of directors has many strengths. First, there will be a large number of financial and prayer supporters that will be very involved in the evangelistic ministry. This will allow the evangelist to be involved in everything from overseas crusades to television ministry because he has broadened his base of support. Secondly, he will tend to be more organized because he has to let the board members know what is going on in his work. He must be organized enough to let them share the vision God has given him. This generally results in better revival planning, a strong prayer chain, and much broader outreach for Christ. Thirdly, the evangelist can afford a team, such as a singer, music director, office helpers, administrator, etc.; A good example of this would be the Billy Graham Evangelistic Association.

Yet there are weaknesses to the large board of directors. First, the board of directors may want the organization to go in a different direction than the evangelist feels led of God to go. While this

---

[2]Not having tax exempt status gives rise to another weakness, relating to the home church. If people desire tax-exempt credit for their contributions, then it will be necessary for gifts to the evangelist to be funneled through his home church. This should not be a problem, but on occasion some home churches will not want to handle this money. If the evangelist had a Not-For-Profit organization, the funds would not have to go through a church treasury.

scenario rarely happens, when it does it is an almost unbearable situation. Secondly, a great deal of time must be spent in sending out newsletters, cultivating board members, having board meetings and banquets. (It is worth the trouble.) Thirdly, the cost of postage, and keeping an office is very expensive. However, a broad enough support-base will compensate for these needs. Associates can be hired to handle administrative tasks as well as workers to handle everything from mail to television cameras. Fourthly, the CPA fees and tax papers that must be filed with the IRS are staggering. All the paper work increases drastically.

The evangelistic association with a small board of directors (from 5 to 7) has strengths, too. The strength of a small board of advisors lies mainly in the fact that the evangelist can more easily maintain control of his organization by hand picking the small board members. Secondly, the cost of operation is less than the large board. The board can be called on short notice and business can be handled swiftly. Thirdly, everything the large board can do, the small board can do. In fact, one of the largest evangelistic associations in the world uses this small board organization.

There has been much criticism of one large evangelistic association, which has family as its directors. Only the family knows where the money goes. This criticism could be overcome with a full disclosure of their finances annually. Secondly, when the financial support base is small, fewer people are involved in decision-making, and normally fewer people pray. Annual banquets or a large non-voting advisory boards can overcome these deficits.

All three forms of these organizations have been shown to work well according to God's blessing. Honesty, integrity, and the leadership of God are a must in all three.

By June 1974, Keith was sure of God's call into itinerant-revival evangelism. Many fellow students knew God was dealing with him and using him in this area during both college and seminary years. In fact, the last eight week's term prior to graduating from New Orleans Baptist Theological Seminary, Keith preached eight revivals. In early

July, he went to Sal Tardo's Barber Shop to get a haircut. Coming down the narrow stairway that led up to Sal's barber chair was a man whose spirit bore witness with his spirit. Keith spoke to him in passing. Later that day Keith ran into him in the Baptist Book Store on the New Orleans Campus. They shared testimonies and Keith told him about God's call in his life. This man's name was Leo Humphrey. God was using him mightily in a soul-winning ministry on Bourbon Street. Leo told Keith about his organization and advised him to start an evangelistic association with a small, trusted board of advisors.

How to Start an Evangelistic Association:

Keith explains how he got his start:

"I asked Leo Humphrey how to set up a Not-For-Profit organization (IRS 501(c)3). He told me first to get a charter for the association, and then file Form 1023 with the IRS. He even gave me the name of a lawyer in New Orleans to help me get the charter. So, the Keith Fordham Evangelistic Association, Inc. was chartered in the State of Louisiana in 1974.

"The next obstacle was the filling out of Form 1023. The lawyer drew up By-laws that included Christian education as a purpose so that I could be further educated, or educate my children on the road with a full tax exemption from the government. However, the lawyer stated that he did not know how to fill out the tax form and advised me to contact a tax lawyer. The tax lawyer said that he knew very little about this type Not-For-Profit organization. In fact, he told me that it took two years for one man to get tax-exempt status and another never did get the status. The Lord intervened again by putting it on the heart of a fellow seminary student, Gary Bowlin, to complete the tax forms. He had been a certified public accountant in Mississippi and had gotten favorable rulings on difficult questions with the IRS. Gary completed the papers in September and within two months I got a phone call from Will Blakemore of the IRS in Texas. He said that I needed to send him a doctrinal statement of beliefs, and I would be given probationary tax-exempt status. That automatically meant I would receive permanent tax-exempt status when the probation period was over."

The laws for Not-For-Profit Organizations vary from state to state and from year to year. However, a number of evangelists have used copies of the "Keith Fordham Evangelistic Association, Inc.'s Charter", Bylaws, Statement of Faith, and the original 1023 tax form to successfully start their evangelistic associations. Consequently, copies of the charter, by-laws, and statement of faith are included in the appendixes.

Here is a summary of some of the steps described:

- Contact a lawyer to find out the state forms needed to establish a Not-For-Profit (these are generally done county by county following state laws);
- In order to complete this filing you will need Articles of Incorporation and By-Laws, see those provided by Keith in the Appendixes;
- Once you have received incorporation status with your county and state, you will then need to file for IRS 501(c)3 status;
- Once this is received, you will then need to file with the state for state tax exempt status;
- Tom incorporated Evangelism Unlimited in Illinois, and then registered Evangelism Unlimited as a foreign entity in three states where he resided, one of these states requires an annual financial report, even though he is no longer a resident of that state, nor does he keep an office in that state. If he does not report to that state attorney general, he will not be allowed to raise funds in that state (Their reminder letter is sitting right next to the computer at this writing);
- Further, in order to maintain financial integrity with tax laws, Evangelism Unlimited uses a payroll service which pay all the appropriate county, state, and federal payroll taxes;
- Please advise yourself of the process state-by-state, county-by-county.

Please remember, in all this administrative intrigue, that your purpose is souls. Your message is the Gospel. But you must innovate and be aggressive. If God has called you, then you must do the work of an evangelist. And if this means starting one or more organizations, by all means, do it!

CHAPTER SIX

THE EVANGELIST AND HIS LOCAL CHURCH

"The evangelist needs the local church, and the local church needs the evangelist. In God's spiritual economy, each needs the other to fulfill the Great Commission."

Tom Johnston

A relationship that adorns the Gospel and the church with beauty and power is that of an evangelist and his home church. When that relationship is going well, the church is going well. When there is no such relationship, the church suffers. While it is clear that each local church needs a pastor to survive, this same need is not often considered of an evangelist. But Ephesians 4:11 clearly lists the evangelist as a necessary leader in the New Testament church. The relationship is reciprocal: every New Testament church needs an evangelist, and every evangelist needs a home church.

It is important that the evangelist be intentional in his relationship to his home church and to its pastor. The evangelist needs the pastor, just as much as the pastor needs the evangelist. And the church needs them both.

By virtue of his office, the evangelist must also remain in contact with hundreds of pastors and learn to work alongside of them. For this reason, he needs to understand the local church and the role of the pastor. While he is not a pastor himself, the evangelist needs to work hand-in-hand with pastors. He must guard and nurture his relationship with pastors, and in particular, the pastor of his home church. This can sometimes be complicated, especially if the evangelist has charisma and is a gifted speaker. Not every leader is comfortable in surrounding himself with other gifted men.

Further complicating matters is a confusion of roles. Keith heard when he was in seminary, "You must have the pastor's heart to be an evangelist." However, if a seminarian has a pastor's heart, then it is likely that he is called to be a pastor. Ephesians 4:11 clearly differentiates between the role of a pastor and that of an evangelist. It is more likely that the saying should be, "The evangelist must have the heart of an evangelist!" This heart of an evangelist means that the evangelist is especially concerned that the church be reaching out to lost people in its community while upholding a gospel-friendly environment of vibrant and committed Christianity.

So the evangelist must have a heart for churches and for their pastors. Evangelists ought to appreciate their pastors. They should love pastors. It is through the ministry of the pastor that the God-called evangelist is encouraged to go deeper with the Lord. It is through the pastor and the church that the young evangelist is sent to seminary to study. It is through the church and pastor that the young man is encouraged to keep pressing on when the going gets tough. It is through the local body of Christ that the evangelist will be surrounded with people who will encourage him in developing a ministry of evangelism. It is in meeting other pastors that the travelling evangelist comes to understand the particular needs of each local church in its own community. It is in and through the church that decisions are made for Christ. The local church and its pastor will normally baptize the fruits of the ministry of the evangelist. Further, the pastor and church are called to follow-up and to provide nurture for the harvest that the Lord brings through the urgent ministry of the revival evangelist. The evangelist and the local church need each other to fulfill Christ's Great Commission.

The Pastor in the Spiritual Nurture of the Evangelist

Evangelist Keith Fordham recalled the amazing role that pastors played in his early spiritual development:

"My home pastors have always ministered to me. Dr. Paul Gilliam was pastoring Calvary Baptist Church in Forest Park, GA, when I was saved. In fact, he was using a full-time evangelist to stir the church to witness and to reap a harvest of souls the week I was saved.

"Dr. Gilliam took time with my father to help him to grow spiritually. Dr. Gilliam forcefully preached the Word and guided me toward God. Once he took me to a meeting of young people where a preacher was going to preach especially to youth. I was leading the way into the open-air tabernacle and started to sit in the back. He said, 'No, we must not sit on backsliders row; we need to get close where the spiritual spout of blessings comes out. If God leads us to make a decision, we will be close and have no barriers to coming.' He preached from the Old Testament giving me a love for the Bible. He knew God was calling me to preach and he encouraged me.

"When he died, God sent Rev. F. J. Hendrix as our interim pastor. He took up where Dr. Gilliam had left off. He, too, knew God had called me to preach. He licensed me to preach and sent me to Samford University in Birmingham. He advised me to finish college before getting married, and then to go on to seminary.

"God then gave Rev. Bill Thomas to me as pastor. Brother Thomas allowed me to preach over fifty times while in college. He kept me on fire for preaching and taught me soul winning. He would drive me around Forest Park and see a group of boys playing a pickup game of football or basketball. He would drive onto the field of play get out of the car and say, 'Boys come here, you know Keith Fordham, you watched him carry the ball on Friday nights. He has something he wants to tell you.' Often we would see between 2 and 6 saved as I shared the gospel. He gave me on the job training in how to draw the net. He ordained me, used me as a youth director, and later performed our wedding.

"It was my privilege during college and seminary to serve on staff with Larry Wimberly in Birmingham and Frank Gunn in Biloxi, MS. The pastors in the churches where I was a member of while at Samford and New Orleans (not on the church staff) were a blessing to my wife and me, although we were members only briefly. The churches afforded me opportunities to go soul-winning on visitation night and work with various groups in the church."

Oh, the joys of spiritual growth in the local church. What a blessing it is when a pastor pours his heart and soul into the lives of others, and sees young men like Keith Fordham grow like olive shoots under their spiritual care. But this ministry of encouragement does not stop with a call to ministry. It continues on.

The Church Sends Out the Evangelist

The local church is not only the avenue for blessing and spiritual growth for the young believer, it is also the avenue upon which his ministry is founded, funded, and sent out. Much like the Acts 13 pattern, in which the Antioch church sent off Barnabas and Paul, so the local church today is involved in sending out workers into other harvest fields to labor. Such is the case for the evangelist. Keith Fordham explained the encouragement and support of Ash Street Baptist Church in Forest Park, Georgia:

"In 1974, I became an itinerant, revival evangelist. God led me to join Ash Street Baptist Church in Forest Park. Charlie Thompson, Jr. was pastor. The church offered a full program of choirs, Sunday School, G.A.s (Girls in Action) for my daughter, and had a tremendous youth program. I knew that while I was travelling as an evangelist, my family would be well ministered to spiritually. Furthermore, when I came home I could hardly wait to sit at my pastor's feet. I was like an empty sponge needing to be filled with the Word of God. From that day to this my home pastors have not failed me in the pulpit. Rev. Woodrow Hudson encouraged me in the Lord. My brother Lane answered the call to preach under his preaching. Even though Brother Hudson has gone on to other fields of ministry, he continued to recommend me, use me, and encourage me. Pastor Joey Hancock was in evangelism for a time and knew of my needs. He served as Pastor-Advisor for the Conference of Georgia Baptist Evangelists and led our church to include me in their budget. "Ash Street Baptist Church was

81

my home church. The church is a source of blessing, comfort, warmth, love, and encouragement in my life. For thirteen years they provided their facilities for my annual banquet. For several years Sarge Allen cooked the banquet meal, along with some of the finest men and women that God has ever placed on this earth. When Sarge went home to be with the Lord, the Brotherhood of the church stepped in and began to cook. The ladies would decorate and help serve at the banquet.

"The most wonderful thing Ash Street did was to refer to me as 'our evangelist.' They allowed me to go with the youth group on mission trips for the Home Mission Board and preach and 'draw the net' in the night meetings. They commissioned me to go overseas by a special time of prayer. Just before going to India in 1987, I was called to the front of the church where I knelt down while the men of the church prayed for me. The pastor led in a beautiful prayer and I felt the power of God in my life. On Wednesday nights, the church included me on the prayer calendar. I feel the power of God in an unusual way on days when the church prays for me. They prayed for me and for the team of men with me while we were preaching in India. They prayed that we would see more than 10,000 people saved during each of the three Wednesdays that we were there. God answered their prayers and many more. When Ash Street prays, God hears and answers. Ash Street was a source of spiritual strength and power in my life.

"That 'welcome home' feeling I felt, along with the handshakes and words of encouragement came from ever quarter of the church. My pastor, at the time, was Joey Hancock. He would ask me to report to the church about our work periodically. Normally, I would do this at prayer meeting. However, he occasionally had me share in the Sunday morning service.

"I was also used as a supply preacher. The people of the church recommend me to other churches. The church put me in the budget. They paid my health insurance. They gave me $3,600 a year (in 1987), and they held my banquet in conjunction with the Mid-Winter Bible Conference. This allowed me to utilize some of the top speakers in the convention at very little cost to my ministry, because the church provides an excellent offering for these men. Brother Joey Hancock had men like Dr. Roy Fish of Southwestern Seminary, Fred Wolfe of Mobile, and Evangelist Sam Cathey to be the speakers at my banquet.

Lois Jane, Jay McKay, Hubert Greer, the Jim Bob Griffin Family, Ron and Claudia Henderson, and others were guest singers.

"Individual members of the church helped me financially, some occasionally and some regularly. Without this support it would have been impossible for me to continue to grow in effectiveness. Yes, I love all local churches, because I love my home churches. Ash Street and now Harp's Crossing recognize God's call on my life and affirm me in my ministry of evangelism."

It is great to read of the experiential blessing that an evangelist derives from being a member of a local church. All these come from submission to the authority of the local church and developing a good relationship with its pastor.

The Pastor and the Evangelist Holding Each Other Accountable

As we look at Ephesians 4:11, we notice that the evangelist and the pastor are colleagues in the work of God. Further, it appears from experience that this collegial relationship is best served by mutual accountability. In the old days, I am told, every Southern Baptist pastor was encouraged to have his evangelist, and every evangelist was encouraged to have his pastor.

Tom was privileged to develop such a relationship with Dr. David Butler at Springdale Church in Louisville, Kentucky. We would meet every week for an hour of fellowship and prayer. It became one of my favorite hours each week, and I dearly missed those times of fellowship when we moved to the Kansas City area. In that relationship I learned several things. First, I learned that a pastor appreciated rubbing shoulders with an evangelist to help him keep accountable in soul-winning. It is not surprising that the pressures of a growing church can easily push soul-winning to the back burner for the pastor. A weekly time when a pastor meets with a God-called evangelist can keep soul-winning in the forefront of his mind. Second, a relationship between a pastor and evangelist keeps the evangelist accountable for his use of time, his preaching and his teaching, as well as his relationship to the church. Third, a

83

relationship between a pastor and evangelist can provide each of them mutual accountability and a sounding board in moral, spiritual, missional, and doctrinal issues.

Since 1988, Dr. J. Dennis Watson has been Keith's pastor. He is an incredible blessing. He nominated Keith as a vice president of the Georgia Baptist Convention and he won. Later in the chapter I will enumerate the role that J. Dennis Watson and Harp's Crossing play in keeping me on the road for Jesus.

Keith, for his part, told me that his pastor has become his best friend. More than anyone else (outside of his own family), his pastor, Dr. J. Dennis Watson of Harp's Crossing Baptist Church in Fayetteville, Georgia, calls him each Sunday morning to find out where he is preaching. Then at the end of each morning service he leads the entire church in prayer for a harvest of souls where Keith is in revival that week, along with prayer for the ministry of their music evangelist, David Akin. How they appreciate knowing that their home church is praying for them.

Keith and his pastor read the same books and discuss their content by phone. They also study Scripture together by phone. When Keith is back home, he meets with the staff of his home church for lunch on Tuesdays. It provides him the friendship and encouragement of a group of workers in the harvest with whom to be related. The staff of his home church has become a spiritual family to him.

Types of Relationships between an Evangelist and his Local Church

As mentioned above, the local church is like a pool or pond which provides life and vitality to those who are thirsty and in need of fellowship and encouragement. Is this not the case for the God-called evangelist? He needs the support and encouragement that is best provided by a local body of believers who are under the leadership of an evangelistic pastor.

John Bisagno in his book *How to Build an Evangelistic Church* explained how his church worked with evangelists:

"Many of these men are new to the field of evangelism and have extra time during the early years of their ministry. Nearly every evangelist has some time off around May, June, December, January, and February, the slower months for revival meetings. With varying degrees of actual church relationships, the talents and services of the full-time evangelist can be used in the program of the local church.

"In Del City, Oklahoma, we had seven full-time Southern Baptist evangelists and three full-time evangelistic singers. It was our pleasure to recommend, support, and pray for these men, listen to the reports of their meetings when they were home, and minister to their families in their absence. We furnished all ten of them with free stationery, a free office, and hopefully some status in the secular world by being a staff evangelist in an established church rather than being an independent evangelist. And oh, how God blessed us for that! It would be impossible to measure the blessings that came to us for doing it. It was our plan to eventually pay for the health insurance and retirement program of these men as well. From time to time during their off-weeks, they were hired by our church to assist in revival visitation, hospital visitation, prospect visitation, and for baptism follow-up visitation. Fifteen dollars per day or one hundred dollars per week may not be a lot of money, but it can be a great blessing to an evangelist who may be off a few weeks without a meeting at Christmas time and he will certainly be a blessing to you and your church. Through the years we have tried to help the evangelist. We have used them and it has been mutually beneficial to them and to us. God has blessed us for being a blessing to his good men, the evangelists. 'Go thou and do likewise.'"[1]

Brother Bisagno hit on some very practical points. How is the church to relate to the evangelist in matters of financial support? There are four ways that the evangelist can relate to the local church: (1) Staff evangelist, (2) "Our evangelist," (3) Church member only, and (4) No relationship with a home church.

---

[1]John R. Bisagno, *How to Build an Evangelistic Church* (Nashville: Broadman, 1971), 151-52.

Staff Evangelist

As staff evangelists, some are allotted twenty to twenty-six weeks a year for revival outside of the church field. The rest of the year they serve on the church staff as staff evangelists. They head up the visitation program of the church, and are paid a full salary for the weeks they are at home and have full benefits of the secretary, office, insurance, and retirement (etc.) from their home church. Some of the strengths of this method are:

- The evangelist is able to be home with his family more;
- The church has an extra part-time staff member to aide in outreach;
- A new evangelist has more staying power in the work because he has a financial base;
- The home church gets to know the evangelist very well.

"Our Evangelist"

The second method is the one Keith presently enjoys. Since 1988, Dr. J. Dennis Watson has been Keith's pastor. He is an incredible blessing. He nominated Keith as a vice president of the Georgia Baptist Convention and he won.

Keith is considered as a staff evangelist in name only. He goes out on visitation and attends church when he is home. The church supports him financially, prayerfully, and considers him as their evangelist. He ministers in over 40 churches each year and often preaches up to 50 Sundays a year away from his home church.

They have allowed him to rest and recuperate while he is home. They are such a ministering and giving church. Without asking anything in return, they just want the Gospel of Christ to be spread. They treat Keith as their own missionary to the South, to the country, and to the world. Harp's Crossing Baptist Church gives 12½% of their budget to the Cooperative Program and then goes beyond that to aide their evangelists.

Their stamp of approval by their demonstrated support has many advantages.

- The evangelist is not limited to 30 or less revivals a year;
- The evangelist is free to go on mission trips, because he has some financial backing;
- Every year they have a "Keith Fordham Day" and take up an offering to support his ministry;
- They pay 90% of Keith's health insurance;
- A R.A. (Royal Ambassadors) group was named after Keith, thereby teaching the young men of the church that God calls men to the office of evangelist—further demonstrating the importance of the office of evangelist and the need for all Christians to be evangelistic;
- It provides an affirmation for the hand of God in the evangelist's life;
- It gives an added financial base for the evangelist;
- It adds blessedness to the local church—Jesus said, "It is more blessed to give than receive";
- The recommendation of the church, as well as the pastor, opens more doors for the evangelist;
- The incredible prayers and friendships of the Sunday school teacher and class are good for the spiritual health and physical well-being of the evangelist.

Church Member Only with No Support

Sadly, many evangelists are members of a church, which does not support them with prayer, finances, or the confirmation of God's call in their lives. If such is the case for an evangelist, it would be best for him to find a church that upholds the office of the evangelist.

It appears that the difficulty in this scenario lies either with the pastor who is not actively seeking an evangelist for his church, or with the evangelist who is not seeking out such a pastor. Also, as churches change and as pastors move on, the situation for the evangelist can become more complex. May the Lord continue to raise up a large group of churches actively looking for evangelists they can support.

No Relationship with a Home Church

Perhaps because of its prophetic nature, as well as its innovative and entrepreneurial spirit, one of the dangers lodged in the gifting and calling of the evangelist is to deride local churches and their pastors. This critical posture can make it difficult for the evangelist to be in genuine submission to and relationship with a local church. Perhaps this may lead to true "Lone Ranger" evangelism, where the evangelist has no local church foundation upon which to build.

More blessings of a home church

Since Tom grew up on the mission field, and has been involved in a significant amount of personal evangelism, he has come to understand the importance of the local church for providing well beyond financial support. Being sent by a home church also provides:

- A historic view of the interpretation of Scripture, as well as the version of the Bible that is used by the sending group in any given language;
- A theological foundation as to conversion, Baptism, and the Lord's Supper;
- A community of accountability, spiritual interrelationship, and fellowship; and
- Proper biblical parameters for working with others in evangelism (Matt 10:16).

All the financial and material aspects of being sent out by a local church aside (which doesn't need to be the case), these examples provide a huge array of further reasons why being closely connected to a home church is doctrinally vital—and even urgent. As an evangelist, this has been a particular struggle of mine, as I have languished to find local churches that are focused on fulfilling the Great Commission.

Please, Brother Evangelist, don't get discouraged. Remain submitted to a body of believers where you can learn, grow, and be held accountable.

Yes, we are in a spiritual battle, and part of that battle seems to be for Satan to keep the evangelists disenfranchised from a home church, while distracting local churches so that they do not seek to support their God-given evangelist. Further, there are responsibilities and blessings when this interrelationship is fulfilled following the biblical pattern.

Responsibilities of the Evangelist toward His Home Church

The evangelist should listen to his pastor and support his church with his tithes, offerings, and talents. When the evangelist is home, he is to be active in his home church. Occasionally, Keith's pastor has told him to stay home and go to bed, but he feels like there are too many blessings to be had while witnessing or sitting at his pastor's feet. Complete emotional exhaustion or sickness should be the only times you miss church. You should always uphold your pastor in prayer, in conversation, and before your family. God will prosper you for this.

You should never boast about tomorrow, because you do not know what a day may bring forth. But, there is nothing wrong in telling people what God is doing in your home church. Honor Christ by telling others about your favorite church—your home church! You will call on others to move their church letter and become active in the church where you are ministering. Live what you preach and enjoy the church God has put you and your family in.

We long for the day when churches will pay the base salary of evangelists, provide office and secretarial help for them, and provide insurance and retirement for evangelists. Then their offerings from revivals can be plowed back into evangelistic campaigns at home and abroad, where financing is not available. Imagine the potential of an overflow of funds used to spread the Good News!

The blessings of a home church as it relates to an evangelist are unlimited. If you are a pastor or member of a church fortunate enough to have a bona fide God-called evangelist in your church, seek out ways to improve, help, and grow his ministry. Remember that very few churches have an evangelist as a member of their church. Do not forget that God places a responsibility along with every privilege. Seek God's will in this matter.

Many evangelists have been so independent and have had to make it on their own so long that they have missed the blessings of their home churches. Likewise, many home churches have not shared in the wonderful ministry of an evangelist. That does not have to be the case, especially in the Southern Baptist Churches.

CHAPTER SEVEN

FAITH AND FINANCES:
BEST PRACTICES FOR THE EVANGELIST

"God provides the air we breathe, our strength and our finances. He even provides jobs and retirement income. God does it His way and we should never usurp His provision by providing our own way."

Keith Fordham

While the Bible does say, "Man shall not live by bread alone" (Deut 8:3), it does not say, "Man shall not live by bread." Even Jesus, after He quoted Deuteronomy 8:3 to the devil received the ministry of the angels who cared for His physical needs. Further, Jesus had a group of women who traveled with him and cared for His physical needs, as well as for those of His disciples (Luke 8:1-3). Yet, one of the most trying aspects in the life of the evangelist is that of providing for his family.

Keith wrote:

"Above all, the evangelist's lifestyle must be a life of faith. Although a few evangelists sky-rocket into a successful ministry overnight, by far the majority of itinerant, revival evangelists in the Southern Baptist Convention have a tremendous financial struggle during their first five years. It takes time to develop spiritually and to have a name of good report. A man's reputation builds over the years. This shows the wisdom of God and His hand guiding the evangelist. If a man is faithful in small things, then God will allow him to be faithful in large things."

Some take Christ's command to His disciples in Matthew 10 or Luke 9 and 10 as indicative of His desire for evangelists today. In Luke 9:3 we find, "Take nothing for the journey...." In Luke 10:4 we read, "Carry neither money bag, knapsack, nor sandals." If these commands are followed without an understanding of their biblical context: (1) God can and will provide for his servant who is acting in faith, even with a certain level of ignorance; (2) The evangelist living in this way is not living with the fullness of the blessings of obedience that God has communicated in His Word.

Later Jesus amended this command to His disciples just before His crucifixion:

> "And He said to them, 'When I sent you without money bag, knapsack, and sandals, did you lack anything?' So they said, 'Nothing.' Then He said to them, 'But now, he who has a money bag, let him take *it*, and likewise a knapsack; and he who has no sword, let him sell his garment and buy one'" (Luke 22:35-36).

So, at first it may appear in Luke 9 and 10 that the evangelist is to secure no human means of financial support (a Vow of Poverty, if you will). However, contextually, Jesus was teaching His disciples the blessing of receiving from those who are being evangelized (or "Reverse Servant Evangelism," if you will). Later, however, in Luke 22, Jesus commanded His evangelists to take their wallet or money purse with them.

But, some questions naturally follow:

- Is bringing along a wallet relying on God to provide for our every need?
- Did not Paul write, "And my God shall supply all your need according to His riches in glory by Christ Jesus" (Phil 4:19)?
- Does relying on God mean that we ought not to work and therefore act as busybodies (2 Thess 3:10-12)?
- Were not Barnabas and Paul sent out to do the work of God (Acts 14:26)?

Herein we find the issue which must be solved in the mind of every evangelist starting out:

- Ought I to seek to support myself?
- How am I going to support myself?
- And if I do seek support for a ministry of evangelism, how is that going to look?

If an evangelist is married and has a family the issues are far more complex:

- Is it okay for my wife to work outside the home to support me in my ministry of evangelism?
- Is that not relinquishing my duty as a husband and provider?
- Should I step out in faith expecting that God will miraculously provide? Or...
- Should I rely on human means to provide for my family, such as in founding a Not-For-Profit evangelistic organization?

The specific context of each evangelist will differ depending on his cultural context, his church context, the frequency and types of ministry opportunities God places before him, his marital status, and the number of children for which he must care. The Bible does say, when speaking of caring for widows, "But if anyone does not provide for his own, and especially for those of his household, he has denied the faith and is worse than an unbeliever" (1 Tim 5:8). For this reason, as well as because of the comments of Jesus in Luke 23:35-36, it is our belief that the evangelist should be primarily supported by the gifts of God's people.

This chapter provides the necessary "how-to's" the financial side of the ministry of the evangelist, from the perspective of the evangelist, as well as from the perspective of the pastor and church. The wise evangelist will learn from those that have gone before him.

1. The Generous Soul Will Be Blessed

A lesson that every evangelist must learn is that Jesus meant what He said, "It is more blessed to give than to receive" (Acts

20:35). I know of no ministry where this is truer than that of the evangelist.

If Keith helps another evangelist get a meeting, or get on a State Evangelism Conference, or get into the best church in the Convention, then he receives a blessing—not just spiritually either. If a fellow evangelist preaches at First Baptist of Dallas, then he makes it possible for another evangelist to be there one day. If a fellow evangelist speaks on the Georgia State Evangelism Program, and does a good job, then that will pave the way for another evangelist to be on the program one day. Consequently, I pray hard for God to bless my fellow evangelists!

If an evangelist recommends a pastor to a church, and that church calls him, the evangelist will generally end up preaching several revivals at that church. Consequently, we want every pastor we know to have the greatest possible opportunities for God. Is it not the will of God for ministers to love each other, pray for one another, and with all their hearts try to help better their fellow ministers of the Gospel?

This principle is also true in the pastor's life. When he takes an offering for the evangelist, he must realize the financial needs of the evangelist and take the best offering possible. In so doing, he not only ensures a greater harvest around the world, but he teaches his people to respect the office of evangelist. Further, he will increase the respect of his people for the office of pastor and will gradually teach them in a roundabout way to take care of all of God's men, not only evangelists, but also the pastor of their church.

2. Understanding the Needs of the Evangelist

What are the needs of an evangelist? It will vary from man to man, but in 2012 the average offering for a week should be at least $2,500 during key revival weeks. The key revival weeks are from the middle of February through the third week of May, most weeks in August and certainly the week after Labor Day on through the week of Thanksgiving. When can a small church use the evangelist? A wise pastor from a small church can use the evangelist in December, January, early February, June, or July. His church's best offering may not reach $2,500, but during these "off-times" the pastor can obtain some of the top evangelists in the Convention.

Although somewhat dated, Keith has listed his actual contributions and expenditures for his ministry in 2001—in order that you might see some of the expenses involved in being a full-time vocational evangelist:

Keith Fordham Evangelistic Association

2001 Balance Sheet

Income:

Church Offerings/Contributions	55,936.32
Individuals' Contributions	38,822.00
Video Tapes	2,698.00
Other organizations/Refunds/Designated	2,457.83
Total Receipts	99,914.15

Expenses:

Salary (Keith)	35,600.00
Travel	9,122.47
Utilities and housing	16,011.93
Loan repayments	9,141.96
Office, publicity, printing	9,686.98
Postage	4,458.10
Payroll taxes	4,546.99
Retirement	4,800.00
Medical-Dental Insurance	1,584.00
Education	6,240.01
Disability Insurance	1,080.96
Video Tapes	575.58
Dues (Professional)	75.00
Bank Charge for returned check	5.00
Total Expenses	102,928.98

Income-Expenses .... (3,014.83)

By the grace of God, His provision in some banner years allowed him to have enough money in the bank to carry his 2001 budget in the black.

Most evangelists prefer that the pastor take a faith offering. However, some churches are not mature enough to take a true faith offering, and do not make an attempt to meet the evangelist's needs. In such cases, the pastor should have a set amount above the expenses of the meeting and take at least two nights of faith offering to supplement the honorarium. In time, the church will learn that they "cannot out-give God." Not much is written on how to take a love offering. However, John Bisagno has written an excellent chapter in his book *The Power of Positive Evangelism* (please see the appendixes).

3. Working with an Evangelist

The area of finances is closely tied to how the evangelist is treated. This treatment begins with how he is invited, how his expenses are paid to get to the church or location, how he is treated when he is there, what kind of love offering is provided to him, and when the love offering is provided to him—before he leaves. Each of these kindnesses demonstrate respect for the man of God.

- **Inviting the Evangelist**

The wise pastor invites the evangelist at least six months in advance. Some pastors work as far ahead as two years. If the evangelist is to be invited in advance, there are certain things that the pastor must know: (1) The date of the revival; (2) The type of revival: area wide revival, open-air meeting, simultaneous crusade, youth emphasis, evangelistic, deeper life, etc.; (3) The evangelist best suited for the situation. Different evangelists have different approaches, but all of them are used of God.

The pastor's invitation to the evangelist should be personal and courteous, not demanding, but respectful. In the invitation the pastor may state how the Holy Spirit has laid the evangelist on his heart, and how prayer is now being offered that his schedule might permit him to work with his particular church. This first letter initiates the pastor's relationship with the evangelist, therefore, it ought to be courteous and thoughtful. Spell out all details such as date, time, financial arrangements, other team members needed, and the purpose of the revival. It is usually best to let the evangelist suggest the other team members to be invited.

- **Offering**

Budget all revival expenses, including travel, lodging, meals, promotion, etc. Don't take this out of the love offering. Also, avoid revival expense offerings. Budget well in advance so you take only one offering per service, and that being a love offering for the evangelist and his team.

Expenses: Soon after the evangelist has arrived, ask him for his expenses or the amount of his plane fare. Ask the treasurer to make a check for the travel expenses and give it to them early in the week. In some cases you may want to send the evangelist his plane tickets in advance. Some churches also provide cash to cover the evangelist's meal expenses during his stay at the church field.

Love Offering: All of the love offerings should be divided between the preacher and singer (often divided 60:40). It is usually best not to take travel expenses, lodging and meals out of the love offering.

- **Guard His Time**

The wise pastor discovers the evangelist's hobbies and plans to give him time for rest during the week. "All work and no play make the evangelist a dull preacher." The pastor may have one of his laymen take the evangelist hunting, fishing or golfing if he cannot personally do so.

The pastor should not expect the evangelist to make every visit with him. He has not been invited to serve as the pastor's shadow. Many men are unable to do their best at night for having done so much during the day. Time for prayer, study and rest is imperative. Let him spend his time witnessing to prospects, not visiting hospitals and nursing homes. Many pastors have found that visitation of prospects by appointment is most productive.

The pastor should remember that the evangelist has not come to solve his personal or church problems. No evangelist should be expected to say anything from the pulpit that the pastor himself could not say.

4. Church Leader, Practice Integrity in the Use of Funds

Evangelist Billy Graham's name is almost synonymous with integrity, especially as it relates to finances. In fact, Tom heard Cliff Barrows speak of a meeting Billy Graham had with his team in 1946. At this meeting Graham asked his team members to list all the ways in which evangelists had fallen before them. The team came together and they distilled the following four areas of indiscretion:

1. Sexual immorality;
2. Exaggerating numbers (converts or those in attendance);
3. Speaking against the Lord's anointed;
4. Financial indiscretion.

After Graham had listed these things before his team, he told them that these were the things that they were to pray against in their entire ministry. By the grace of God, God protected Billy Graham and his team from these areas of indiscretion for over 65 years. Praise the Lord for His faithfulness as demonstrated through Billy Graham!

May the evangelist be warned. Temptation to financial indiscretion comes with the territory. Take heed and watch out. Pray against it, and order the policies and procedures of your organization likewise. Jesus said, "He who *is* faithful in *what is* least is faithful also in much; and he who is unjust in *what is* least is unjust also in much" (Luke 16:10). Whether you have a small budget or a large budget, show yourself to be a man of integrity at every level.

The following are some proposed recommendations in the use of funds:

- Maintain checks and balances on all use of corporate funds;
- Never allow administrative procedures to allow you to exercise absolute control over any accounts;
- Always clearly report the finances of your organization;
- Never do things in secret; always assume that every transaction will be visible for all to see (Luke 8:17, "For nothing is secret that will not be revealed, nor *anything* hidden that will not be known and come to light");
- Always use funds exactly for that for which they are given or designated. When this becomes impossible (such as the trip for which funds were given has already taken place), then Board action is needed to reallocate those funds;
- Watch raising funds for particular projects when you know that the viability of the project is questionable;
- Be prompt in sending out gift receipt letters;
- Be timely and honest in complying with all federal, state, and local reporting;
- Respect all givers as though they are widows, and all gifts as though they are the widow's last mite.
- Pray regularly for your donors, thanking God for them and for their generosity, and asking God to bless them, prosper them, and protect them and their assets.

Although not always easy, if you do these things you will save yourself a lot of grief in the future!

4. Preliminary Ideas for Fund Raising:

This section is not meant to be a course in fund raising. Rather it is to give ideas for fund raising based on our combined experience of over 70 years in evangelism. Again, the situation will differ drastically depending on your situation. The following are some suggestions:

- Speak to your pastor to share with him how the Lord is leading in your life; his support early on is vital!
- Go forward to make public your decision to be a full-time vocational evangelist;
- Kick-off your ministry of evangelism with a dinner at your home church; make this an annual part of your ministry;
- Gather together a mailing list of people who are interested in staying in contact with you at the dinner, by having them fill out information on an envelope at their table;
- Gather together people who can form the board for a Not-For-Profit corporation in the county of your home church, until Not-For-Profit status is received, your home church may allow funds to be sent through them (consider having a lawyer and accountant on the board);
- Get into the habit of sending out a prayer letter every month, with a giving envelope for a response; be sure to include an ask in every letter, as well as a response device; sending out a letter before the first of the month will help regular donors give on a monthly basis;
- As special needs or projects come up, be sure to include those as part of your ask;
- Make your prayer needs known in your letters; your needs are spiritual as well as financial.

Further, you will need to develop policies for how you plan to work with local churches or other groups that invite you. Remember that if you wanted to be treated with courtesy and respect, then you should also treat all those who contact you with courtesy and respect. Long-time Evangelist Junior Hill has on his website some basic principles to communicate some of these expectations to those who contact his ministry.

5. Junior Hill's Statement of Principles

Please consider in closing this chapter the "Statement of Principles" from the website of Junior Hill, an esteemed statesmen among Southern Baptist evangelists:

- **PREACHING:** I will to the best of my ability seek to preach those messages the Lord lays upon my heart. While it is likely, as an evangelist, that those messages the Lord most blesses will be repeated in other meetings, I will pray that the Lord will deliver me from preaching "canned sermons". You can rest assured that I will not badger or browbeat your church.

- **DECISIONS:** I am under no compulsion to "produce" decisions and have no record to uphold. I will preach, pray, and visit to the best of my ability and then trust the Lord to give whatever increase he pleases. I promise you there will be no tricks or pressured invitations. They will be clear, to the point, and given in courtesy.

- **VISITATION:** I am coming to be your guest. In any way that I can help you, I want to be used. I will place myself in your hands and will do whatever you desire in this area.

- **MONEY:** Under no circumstances will I promote the offering. The sincere pastor who uses a full-time evangelist will realize the special needs of this calling and will lead the church to give a worthy offering. If the Lord has led you to invite me, He will lead you to know what I need to continue this work. …

- **PASTOR:** If I know my heart, I want to help you as a pastor. One does not spend eleven years in the pastorate without knowing the heartaches, as well as the joys, of this calling. You can rest in full assurance that I will honor and exalt your ministry before your church.[1]

Go and do likewise!

---

[1] "Statement of Principles"; Junior Hill Ministries; available at: http://juniorhillministries.com/Principals.htm (online); accessed 26 June 2012; Internet. Used by permission.

CHAPTER EIGHT

THE LIFE OF THE EVANGELIST

"And He said to them, 'Come aside by yourselves to a deserted place and rest a while.' For there were many coming and going, and they did not even have time to eat."

Mark 6:31

Can you imagine that the Son of God came to earth, who upholds all things by the word of His power, was so caught up in His ministry with people that He did not have time to eat! If it happened to the Son of Man, it can and will happen to us, who follow in His footsteps.

The lifestyle of the evangelist, particularly in his early years of ministry, as financial necessity coupled with the promise of God's provision, along with the cry of dying souls, can drive him to exhaustion. Jesus told Peter, "The spirit is willing but the flesh is weak" (Mark 14:38). Paul also recognized the weakness of his own flesh, as he explained the Corinthian church how he dealt with his own body:

> "But I discipline my body and bring *it* into subjection, lest, when I
> have preached to others, I myself should become disqualified"
> (1 Cor 9:27).

The subjugation of one's own body is no laughing matter. In fact, a lack of discipline in this area can disqualify an evangelist from that to which he is called, preaching!

Jesus said, "But seek first the kingdom of God and His righteousness, and all these things shall be added to you" (Matt 6:33). But what are "these things"? "'What shall we eat?' or 'What shall we drink?' or 'What shall we wear?'" (Matt 6:31). Armed with these and many other verses, young evangelists may feel, as we did and do, that because of this command, coupled with further urgencies in Scripture, the real issue is not a lack of God's provision, the real issue is our absolute obedience. And they are correct in this assertion!

Further, notice some of the terminology of Jesus when He told His disciples to go forth. He said, "When they persecute you in this city, flee to the next" (Matt 10:23). Jesus promised that gospel ministry would not be easy, but rather difficult, even to the point of costing our lives:

> "But beware of men, for they will deliver you up to councils and scourge you in their synagogues. ... Now brother will deliver up brother to death, and a father *his* child; and children will rise up against parents and cause them to be put to death. And you will be hated by all for My name's sake. But he who endures to the end will be saved" (Matt 10:17, 21-22).

So the young evangelist is correct as he is seeking to share the Good News with reckless abandon. Paul said:

> "I do not count my life dear to myself, that I may finish my race with joy, and the ministry which I received from the Lord Jesus, to testify to the gospel of the grace of God" (Acts 20:24).

In the process of this abandonment for the gospel, Jesus also calls on us to use wisdom, even uncanny wisdom:

> "Behold, I send you out as sheep in the midst of wolves. Therefore be wise as serpents and harmless as doves" (Matt 10:16).

We are to use the wisdom of a serpent. This wisdom is primarily commanded in the context of persecution and seeking to share the Gospel with a lost and dying world. Yet it also seems to apply to wise balance in the ministry of evangelism. The lifestyle of the vocational evangelist can be like a pressure cooker.

1. Keith's First Years of Ministry

After graduating from New Orleans Baptist Theological Seminary, Keith went right into full-time evangelism:

"During my first year, I preached Sunday mornings through Friday nights. It was not uncommon for me to drive all night long on Friday to my next preaching assignment. Often, I would drive up to the church, get out of my car at 8:30 to 9:30 a.m. on Saturday morning, go into the bathroom of the church where the revival was to begin on Sunday morning, splash water on my face, and comb my hair. The purpose of this was to wake up enough to teach a 10:00 a.m. Witness Clinic that I held on Saturdays from 10:00 a.m. until noon. At noon we would all take a short break and eat a meal. Then we would go soul winning for two hours. Then, about 2:30 p.m., I would leave the church and go to a bed that I had never slept on before, usually in someone's home. The strange noises, dogs, and children would make sleeping, or even resting, extremely difficult.

"Normally, each new place also meant a new schedule. All this would be enhanced with two meals out a day and a large meal after each evening service. Occasionally, I would have 7:00 a.m. or 10:00 a.m. morning services as well. This would only add to my exhaustion. About every third revival week, the pastor would add to this already hectic schedule with early morning hospital visitation, plus afternoon visitation where we would make many other visits to people who had been neglected since the previous revival.

"Combine all of the above, with the fact that I always seem to stay awake the night before I leave for a new place—just like a child, excited over new people and a new work. You can begin to imagine the physical and mental fatigue which I was experiencing. Then when it was time for me to return home, I would always stay awake the night before—thrilled with the anticipation of a warm reunion with my family. When I finally arrived home, I would often collapse. No one, not even my wife, could understand the condition of my body and emotions. Anyone can drive all night Friday night, stay up all day

Saturday, go into a strange bed and keep up that schedule from one to three weeks without much difficulty, but about the fourth week, a great exhaustion sets in. By the eighth week a man gets his second wind. Then on the twelfth week of continuous revivals he says, 'Push my button when it's time for me to preach.'

"About my fifth year of evangelism, I began to preach Sunday morning through Wednesday or Thursday night meetings. By that time, I had discovered that preaching nineteen or twenty weeks in a row would put me in grave emotional danger—a person can get out of touch with reality! One night after a string of some sixteen revivals, I drove into Forest Park at 2:00 a.m. in the morning. I drove around Forest Park for nearly forty-five minutes. I could not remember where I lived! I pulled over to the side of the road, opened the door, knelt on the ground, and prayed, 'Dear Lord Jesus, please help me find my house.' I put the car in drive and went straight home. For nine years my wife met me at the door. Whether I came home at 2:45 a.m. or 5:00 a.m., she would stay up all night to greet me at the door."

Brother Keith related story after story of the difficulties of missing family and of insomnia when on the road. The life of a traveling evangelist is a grueling and difficult life. Because of the strain and stress, many evangelists turn to another work. Some become pastors. Others get into denominational work in some way. The life of a traveling evangelist is lonely and hard.

2. Pressures to Quit the Work

The pressures of life on the road can be so difficult, that the God-called traveling evangelist will be tempted to settle down to another style of life. Such was the case for Jewish Evangelist Hyman Appelman, who was tempted one day to take a church:

- **Hyman Appelman Turning Down a Pastorate**

"A certain tremendous church wanted me to be their pastor. The pulpit committee met me at the station as I was on my way to New York and said, 'We are going to call you Wednesday night.' I went into that Pullman thanking God, rejoicing that at last, after all these driving, lonely years, I was going to be with my wife and babies in the pastorate of a church I loved, among people whom I knew and loved. Oh, I was thanking God in gratitude, with tears starting down from my eyes and rolling down my cheeks, when in that Pullman, racing through the night at express speed, I had a visit from Jesus. He said, 'Son, why do you want to be a pastor?'

"I said, 'Lord, I am tired. Lord, I am blue. Lord, my nerves are frayed. My mind is ready to crack. I cannot stand any more. I am just tired. I want to be at home with my wife and children for awhile.'

"Jesus said, 'Son, you have forgotten that I was away from home thirty-three years, and I had to die to get back home.'

"Do you know what I did? I put on my clothes and got out of that berth. When the train stopped at the very next station I sent a telegram to those people and said, 'Don't call me; I am not coming. I am just going to keep on with Jesus.' It was a time of testing."[1]

- **The Stress of Leaving Home**

Jack Stanton of Southwest College in Bolivar, Missouri, told Keith that two or three days before he went off to start his revival campaigns, he would "get as mean as the devil." He was irritable just thinking about having to be away from home. Homesickness, not from one day or one week away from home, but from months and years away from home, increases until it becomes unbearable. Rev. Jimmy Coleman was asked years ago when he was in evangelism, "Do you cry when you go off in revival?" He would answer, "Yes, for three days." The pastor asked, "Was this the last three days before you went home?" Jimmy replied, "No, for three days before I left the house."

- **The Need for Rest**

The strain and exhaustion of road life cannot be cured by a three-minute call home every day. Nor can sleeping thirty-six hours straight rest a man from eight to twenty weeks of revival on the road. It has been Keith's personal experience that a full three weeks of

---

[1]Hyman Appelman, "God's Plan for Revival," in Robert J. Wells and John R. Rice, eds., *How to Have Revival, by America's Leading Evangelists* (Wheaton, IL: Sword of the Lord, 1946), 22.

total rest at home can get a man back in shape mentally, physically, emotionally, and spiritually. If three weeks does not work, a man needs professional help.

Three weeks of complete rest may not be possible for the evangelist until he has been in the work full-time for over two or up to three years. Some evangelists take off one week a month. Others preach Sunday through Sunday and are off the next five days until the next meeting. In order to do this a man needs to have a tremendous evangelistic organization or be on the "Home Run Circuit"—that is, preaching in super churches with super offerings. For the average evangelist it may take years to get to this point, and there are many others who never arrive there.

3. Traveling with the Family

In 1983 (after nine years of traveling ministry), under the advice of some godly men, one of which was Keith's pastor, Joey Hancock, he realized that his family needed to travel with him. The years of homesickness and travel weariness had almost overcome him emotionally. Keith purchased a thirty-three foot travel trailer and a 1975 Jeep Wagoneer with a 360 V-8 engine to pull it. Then his family started going with him. Keith has never regretted that step of faith, and neither has his family. God has richly blessed their travels together!

- **The Blessing of One's Wife:**

Every evangelist must realize that when his wife is with him, she is more sensitive to his needs than he is. By being with him, she can know more about him, than he does, and she knows it sooner. When she is not with him every day, it is impossible for her to exercise her God-given helpmate abilities. Evangelist, enlist the help of your wife to prevent you from working yourself into a nervous breakdown. She will help you to get balance and harmony into your life.

- **Living Accommodations**

When an evangelist takes his family with him on the road, he has several options. He can drive or fly and have them stay in a motel with him, or he can purchase a motor home, a travel trailer, or even a fifth wheel.

Living in motels is quite difficult and cost prohibitive for most families. While options now include the "Extended Stay" hotel suites, eating out and entertaining children can be very difficult in a hotel environment. If the evangelist is travelling by himself or with his wife, or if he is only taking short meetings, the hotel or extended stay may be good options. But for weekly travel from church to church, with months away from home, then other options must be considered.

The evangelist, who plans to travel for long periods, going from church to church, may consider purchasing a motor home. A motor home is especially good for couples without children, or for music evangelists who do numerous, one night concerts and move almost continuously. One disadvantage of a motor coach is that you must tow a vehicle behind the coach for driving around town when you arrive at your location. While some churches are in a position to provide a loaned or rental car, most are not. Further, motor coaches lose some living space due to the driving or steering area.

An evangelist travelling with his family may want to purchase a travel trailer. In this case, the tow vehicle serves for daily errands when on site at the church. It must be remembered that the true living space of a travel trailer is actually about 3 feet less than the overall length of the travel trailer, because its length is measured from the ball hitch at the front to the back bumper. When you are living in a trailer up to 150 days a year with two children, every foot counts!

A third type option for mobile lodging is a fifth wheel travel trailer. An additional advantage of the fifth wheel is the space over the hitch assembly is generally used as a bedroom. For years, Keith and Shirley used a 40 foot fifth wheel travel trailer towed by a gas-guzzling truck—with a 454 engine. Gas consumption was one of the negatives of this option. Their truck was a one-ton pick-up truck with four doors and dual wheels on the back axle. By the way, if you are considering a tow vehicle, remember that it is best not to undercut on power. It is always better to burn a little more gas so that you can get where you are going, rather than to have regular breakdowns along the side of the road. Keith's and Shirley's fifth-wheel trailer had two hydraulic glides, providing about three feet of extra width in certain sections. They found that the fifth wheel rig was much easier to handle on the road than their former travel trailer and offered them much more living space upon arrival.

As he has aged, however, the extra effort of towing a trailer and setting it up has become too difficult. At the present time he and his wife travel in a full-size vehicle or minivan unless they fly. With their children grown and out of the nest, it is far easier to stay in motels.

- **GPS Systems, Cellular Phones, Satellite Television, and Mobile Hotspots:**

With the boom in mobile technology, some aspects of life on the road have really changed. For example, GPS systems have made it much simpler to get directions from one place to another. Cell phones coverage is also available on most major highways and in major cities. Mobile hotspots can piggyback on cell phone towers to provide 3G or 4G Internet coverage in many areas of the country. Also, Internet sites, such as Google Maps and MapQuest, provide fairly reliable maps for finding routes to most towns and churches.

This technology boom also provides more cost effective world-wide telephone calling through Skype and similar programs. For those who need to plan board meetings, or need to video chat with pastors, video conferencing is also made easier through sites such as Skype or Oovoo.

Satellite television and digital television have also changed the availability and clarity of television. Because of these recent changes, Christian stations have also become more accessible to potential viewers, which include some excellent shows with quality pastors and evangelists. It must be admitted that Tom rarely watches television anymore. But when his boys are home they sometimes watch sports. But since they are now out of the house, and since they have dropped their satellite television. Watching an old television show or movie on Hulu, news on Fox News or BBC News, or sports on ESPN can provide the necessary downtime that is needed in the hectic pace of traveling ministry.

- **The Importance of Schedules:**

A big bonus of traveling with your wife is sticking to a schedule. A wife and mother are particularly wired for making sense out of chaos, and she must be allowed to do so. There is the chaos of travelling from church to church. There is the potential chaos of providing an education to children. There is the chaos of living in very close quarters with little space to "get away." Your wife will be your primary and most important God-given gift to help make peace out of chaos. One of the important points to maintaining sanity is the need for a daily schedule of activities. These activities include among other things, devotions, eating, studying, exercise, and ministry. Having a routine will keep the travel home a haven, even when it is a home on four, eight, or twelve wheels.

- **Home Schooling:**

An early issue that arises when you consider taking your family on the road is that of schooling for the children. After homeschooling our daughter and son for ten years each, it seemed that everywhere we traveled people wanted to know what we did about our children's schooling. While some states have laws concerning people who teach their children at their home (in a stationary location), it appears that no state prohibits people who travel, such as missionaries, ambassadors, circus people, and even evangelists, from teaching their children on the road.

Further, now a days, there are a large number of websites available for potential homeschoolers to investigate the possibilities and prospects for homeschooling. Some of these are:

- o   http://www.homeeducatorsresource.com/
- o   http://www.sonlight.com/
- o   http://www.home-school.com/
- o   http://www.homeschool.com/

Quite a few churches also have home-school networks of families who home-school their children. As you travel, you will be able to gather and glean information on homeschooling from various churches and locations. You may then become a conduit to provide information to other people in a similar situation.

- •   **Study:**

Another grave danger comes in the area of the evangelist's study. Every Christian must feed on the Word of God. This is especially true of the evangelist. You must receive something before you can give it. Exhaustion and travel can cause your studies to lag, and so can the lack of space for books, devotionals, and notebooks. One way to learn "on the road" is to purchase CDs or use an I-Pod. The entire Bible can be downloaded from I-Tunes or it can be purchased on CD. Books, sermons, or music can be listened to while driving, or in place of watching television when your eyes are desperately in need of rest. Further, there are websites that host the sermons of pastors, as well as the individual church sites of each pastor. If you have a favorite pastor, it is likely that you can download MP3s of his sermons and listen to those as you drive. Digital radio, Sirius radio, and Pandora also provide sources for quiet music during long periods of travel.

A further help in study is to make use of a laptop computer, a tablet, or an I-Pad. These do not take too much space, but can hold Bible software programs such as Accordance, Bible Navigator,

BibleWorks, E-Sword, Logos, PC Study Bible, QuickVerse, or WordSearch. While these Bible software are designed for different platforms (IBM or Apple), they also have different capabilities, libraries, and costs. Tom currently uses BibleWorks, because he is on an IBM platform and likes to check multiple Bibles in multiple languages simultaneously. Logos, on the other hand, appears to have the availability of huge libraries of Bible helps and commentaries. The nice thing about having these in a software format is the availability of word searches of entire libraries with a click of the mouse. All of these are aids to study, but they ought not replace the time for study.

One excellent habit that Tom has developed recently is that of handwriting of Scripture. He is currently handwriting the Book of Romans one verse at a time in French, in two Greek versions, and in Latin. He began handwriting Deuteronomy using an English Bible—based on Deuteronomy 17:18-20. Then he went to handwriting Deuteronomy and alternating daily with the Pauline epistles in the New Testament. This has revolutionized his devotional life, and given him a hunger for the Word of God. As far as traveling goes, it is quite difficult for him to take several three-ring binders, his computer, and several Bibles with him when he travels by car or plane. Yet it has been effective for keeping fresh in Bible study.

As far as outside studies, Keith has studied flying and ventriloquism, graduating from Maher Ventriloquist School, a correspondence school. He has also attended numerous conferences and clinics, and has read many books to further his interests.

Traveling in the trailer with his family greatly improved Keith's study habits. In fact, he began seeking more seminary training because of this change in his schedule. Beforehand a Doctor of Ministry degree seemed completely out of reach. He could not take six months out of his ministry to go to seminary and complete the seminars, much less meet with an advisor once a month on a set day. A revival schedule just would not allow it. Later on in his ministry he did gain that flexibility. Keith then discovered Immanuel Bible

Seminary in Sharpsburg, Georgia. Such notable men as Nelson Price of Roswell Street Baptist, R. G. Lee, and Hyman Appelman had Doctorates from there. He was able to attend the week-long seminars, or watch lectures by videocassette. The intense studies gave him the mental and spiritual stimulation that fueled his passion for souls, and gave him an interest in learning more.

In the last five years especially, online classes and programs have become more common. Although they do require regular Internet access, an online program provides the flexibility that a travelling evangelist needs, while allowing him to study in an area of interest from anywhere that he can access the Internet. As is generally the case in further studies, there is a need for perseverance and discipline to complete an online degree.

- **Internet and Internet Accountability**

While the Internet and technology can be fussy, and sometimes downright frustrating, it provides amazing possibilities. As we noted, the Internet is great for homeschoolers and researchers in general. It also provides the evangelist access to many Bible study tools. However, along with this wealth of information comes the need for accountability. For, while the Internet has almost an unending volume of historical information and Bible research tools, it happens to be that pornographers are the ones who are making the most money with this communicatory tool. Therefore, it is highly recommended, that the evangelist or family planning to make the Internet a regular diet for information, place on their computer some type of accountability or blocking software. Tom uses the accountability software called "Covenant Eyes" to maintain an accountability relationship with his two post-adolescent boys. Because of the growth of the problem of pornography, and because of the pressures of travel, such as software is highly encouraged. Sites such as Focus on the Family provide an array of software available for either blocking noxious content or providing web browsing accountability.

Life on the road is a huge adjustment. If you are married and you are on the road, love your wife, and work closely with her to determine what is the best situation for you and for your family. As long as you love her and listen to her, together you can make it as an evangelist living life on the road.

If you know that God has truly called you, don't give up. Keep fighting the good fight, at home or on the road!

CHAPTER NINE

THE EVANGELIST AND HIS PREACHING

"A sermon without Christ as its beginning, middle and end is a mistake in conception and a crime in execution."

C. H. Spurgeon

The evangelist is commissioned by God to evangelize the evangel. His primary role and his preeminent responsibility is to preach the Gospel. Once he ceases to evangelize, he ceases to be an evangelist!

But what is the essence of the message that he should preach, and how does that relate to the preaching that regularly takes place in the church? It is our opinion, that because of the poor translation of the Greek verb for "evangelize" in the English language, the distinction between preaching and evangelizing has been lost. Not only does this have ramifications as to how the preaching in the church is viewed, but it even has ramifications as to the role and usefulness of an evangelist in the ministry of the church. Therefore, it is difficult to find any book on the church and its function published today, or any theological course on ecclesiology that speaks of the role of the evangelist in and for the local church. No wonder some churches have never used an evangelist!

And it all seems to stem from a poor translation in the English language since Wycliffe's Second edition (1388)!

John Wycliffe had it right in his 1382 translation of the New Testament from the Latin Vulgate. He translated the Latin term *evangelizo* with the English term "evangelize" (36 times, out of the

Vulgate's 43 uses, and out of the Greek's 55 uses of εὐαγγελίζω, *euangelizo*). So, yes, Wycliffe appeared to coin a term in English by borrowing it from the Latin. By the way, most of the important theological terms in our English New Testaments were "borrowed"—terms like "justification" and "sanctification." Therefore, removing these "borrowed" terms vanillafies or neuters the Bible's message.

But something happened to Wycliffe's 1382 translation of the Bible, it was changed. In 1388—four years after the death of Wycliffe, a "second edition Wycliffe" appeared in England. One of the earmarks of this second edition text-type (considering that all this happened before the invention of movable type in A.D. 1455), was the removal of 33 uses of the word "evangelize" from his 1382 edition. The second edition Wycliffe retained the English verb "evangelize" only 3 times.[1]

Now, why does that make any difference at all?

Because, the English verb used in the second edition Wycliffe to replace the verb "evangelize" was the verb "preach." And it appears that this translation has dominated English-language Bibles since that time. This translation issue begs the question: is there not a substantive difference between that which is preached to spiritually lost people so that they may come to Christ, and what is preached to Christians so that they might grow in the Lord? And if so, what is that difference? Perhaps a brief summary may be in order here.

Using the New American Standard Bible (1977) as an example, it used the English verb "preach" 104 times in the New Testament. It used "preach" to translate six (6) different Greek verbs and two (2) nouns in specific contexts. Of these 104 New Testament uses of the verb "preach":

- 50 are from translations of the Greek verb εὐαγγελίζω (*euangelizo*, evangelize).

---

[1]A chart showing all the uses of "evangelize" in about 16 historic versions of the Bible can be found at: www.evangelismunlimited.org.

- 40 are from translations of the Greek κηρύσσω (*kerusso*, proclaim/preach).
- 6 are from uses for the noun κήρυγμα (*kerugma*, kerygma/preaching).
- 4 are from translations the verbs παρακαλέω (*parakaleo*/beside-call/exhort/encourage), προευαγγελίζομαι (*proeuangelizomai*, or pre-evangelize), διδάσκω (*didasko*, teach), πληρόω (*pleroo*, fill/fulfill).
- 1 is supplied for the noun λόγος (*logos*/word).
- 3 are supplied by the translators.

So it can be readily noted that almost half of the uses of the English "preach" in the NASB is from the Greek verb, which could also be translated "evangelize"—thereby providing English readers an exegetical and contextual distinction. Again, a proper understanding the New Testament difference between a pastor "preaching" and an evangelist "evangelizing" is what is at stake.

While some see no role for the New Testament evangelist in the functioning of the local church, others do not make a distinction between New Testament evangelizing and New Testament preaching. Why this dichotomy? Is it not because the distinction is not clear in English Bible translations?

Now, the Holman Christian Standard Bible used the English verb "evangelize" six times:

- Acts 8:25, "Then, after they had testified and spoken the message of the Lord, they traveled back to Jerusalem, **evangelizing** the many villages of the Samaritans."
- Acts 8:40, "Philip appeared in Azotus, and passing through, he was **evangelizing** all the towns until he came to Caesarea."
- Acts 14:7, "And they kept **evangelizing**."
- Acts 14:21, "After they had **evangelized** that town and made many disciples, they returned to Lystra, to Iconium, and to Antioch."

- Acts 16:10, "After he had seen the vision, we immediately made efforts to set out for Macedonia, concluding that God had called us to **evangelize** them."
- Rom 15:20, "So my aim is to **evangelize** where Christ has not been named, in order that I will not be building on someone else's foundation."

In doing so, the HCSB broke the 611-year censorship on the use of the word "evangelize" in English Bibles!

So what could be learned, if the verb "evangelize" was used more prominently as a translation for the Greek εὐαγγελίζω (*euangelizo*) in English Bibles? It appears to us that the first thing that would be noticed is that, while there is some overlap in the meaning and terms, there is also a substantive difference between evangelizing and preaching. Evangelizing is addressing spiritually lost person with the gospel, through which they may ultimately receive a hearing of faith, come under conviction of sin, and respond by repentance and faith in Jesus Christ as the only answer for forgiveness of their sin. In this context, please note 1 Corinthians 15:1-2:

- 1 Cor 15:1-2, "Now I make known to you, brethren, the gospel by which **I evangelized** you, which also you received, in which also you stand, by which also you are saved, if you hold fast the word by which **I evangelized** you, unless you believed in vain."

Evangelizing, in this context, is used specifically as it related to Paul's proclamation to lost Corinthians, to their reception of that message, and to their initial salvation through that message.

Preaching, on the other hand, is more of a generic term for proclamation. It includes evangelizing the lost, but it is more than that. Several verses may suffice to show this point:

- 2 Tim 4:2, "Preach [κηρύσσω, *kerusso*] the word! Be ready in season *and* out of season. Convince, rebuke, exhort, with all longsuffering and teaching."

- 2 Cor 4:5, "For we do not preach [κηρύσσω, *kerusso*] ourselves, but Christ Jesus the Lord, and ourselves your bondservants for Jesus' sake"
- Col 1:28, "And we proclaim [καταγγέλλω, *katangello*] Him, admonishing every man and teaching every man with all wisdom, that we may present every man complete in Christ"

Notice the repeated use of the words "every man" in this last verse! There is, therefore, an overarching aspect of preaching in that it encompasses both the saved and the lost.

Further, twice in the New Testament the words for preaching and evangelizing are used in parallel form:

- Luke 8:1, "And it came about soon afterwards, that He *began* going about from one city and village to another, preaching [κηρύσσω, *kerusso*] and evangelizing [εὐαγγελίζω, *euangelizo*] the kingdom of God; and the twelve were with Him"
- Acts 8:4-5, "Therefore, those who had been scattered went about evangelizing [εὐαγγελίζω, *euangelizo*] the word. And Philip went down to the city of Samaria and *began* preaching [κηρύσσω, *kerusso*] Christ to them."

Thus there is a certain overlap in the terms.

So the preacher preaches, and the evangelist evangelizes. The evangelist evangelizes lost people to bring them to Christ, and the preacher preaches to all men. So why does it appear that the ministry of the evangelist is shunned these days? Does he not have a God-given New Testament role in the local church, which is confirmed with the New Testament use of the Greek verb for "evangelize" 55 times? Yes, his role is more narrow and defined. It is directly tied to preaching the gospel to lost souls, and bringing them to conversion and salvation. Because many churches confuse when conversion takes place,[2] this is probably one major cause of shunning the God-

---

[2]"XXVII. *Of Baptisme.*

"Baptisme is not only a signe of profession, and marke of difference, whereby Christian men are discerned from other that be not christened: but is also a signe of regeneration or newe byrth, whereby as by an instrument, they that receaue baptisme rightly, are grafted into the Church: the promises of the forgeuenesse of sinne, and of our adoption to be the sonnes of

given role of the evangelist, as well as guarding the clear distinction between evangelizing and preaching in the translations, commentaries, and lexicons that they produce!

So, what can be concluded from this discussion? Just as the pastor is important for the local church, and God used that word once in the New Testament (Eph 4:11), so the work of the evangelist is vital for the New Testament church, God using the word three times in His New Testament (Acts 21:8; Eph 4:11; and 2 Tim 4:5). Can we go so far as to say that a local church without an evangelist is not a New Testament church? It sure makes one wonder.

So then, what is the message of the Gospel that is to be on the lips of this evangelist? While there are many contexts and emphases in the New Testament, the clearest and most potent summaries of the gospel message are found in 1 Corinthians 15:3-5 and Luke 24:46-47. Consider for example Table 6. From these two texts, several points can be made. First, the message of the death of Christ for sin, and his resurrection are important parts of the gospel. Second, notice that his death is for sin. Sadly, the word "sin" was removed in relation to the only reason for Christ's death in Apostle's Creed, "Suffered under Pontius Pilate," and the Nicene Creed, "and was crucified also for us under Pontius Pilate." Yet, the sin problem was central to Paul's presentation of the Gospel in the Book of Romans. Third, Jesus in Luke 24 emphasized the core of the message of the gospel, as well as its necessary response by using the words "repentance and remission of sins will be preached in His name...."

These summaries of the Gospel correspond with the primary points of Paul's message of the Gospel as found in the Book of Romans. It all goes back to Paul's use of the verb εὐαγγελίζω (*euangelizo*) in Romans 1:15, part of the four verses that make up the thematic verses of the entire book. Therefore, (1) εὐαγγελίζω

God, by the holy ghost, are visibly signed and sealed: fayth is confyrmed: and grace increased by vertue of prayer vnto God.

"The baptisme of young children, is in any wyse to be retayned in the Churche, as most agreable with the institution of Christe" ("42 and 39 Articles of Religion"; from: http://www.episcopalian.org/efac/1553-1572.htm; accessed: 21 Oct 2004).

TABLE 6: Comparison of 1 Corinthians 15:3-5 and Luke 24:46-47

	1 Cor 15:3-5	Luke 24:46-47
Preamble	For I delivered to you first of all that which I also received:	Then He said to them, "Thus it is written,
Death of Christ	that Christ died for our sins according to the Scriptures	and thus it was necessary for the Christ to suffer
Burial of Christ	and that He was buried,	
Resurrection of Christ	and that He rose again the third day according to the Scriptures,	and to rise from the dead the third day
Witnesses of resurrection	and that He was seen by Cephas, then by the twelve.	
Message of the Gospel		and that repentance and remission of sins should be preached in His name
Geographic extent		to all nations, beginning at Jerusalem

[*euangelizo*, evangelize] is the main verb for the message of the entire Book of Romans; and (2) εὐαγγελίζω [*euangelizo*, evangelize] provides the link between the evangelizing going on in the Book of Acts, and the message of that evangelizing, from the pen of the Apostle Paul! The ramifications are astounding, and yet not that unexpected.

- Rom 1:15, "Thus, for my part, I am eager to evangelize [εὐαγγελίζω, *euangelizo*] among you also who are in Rome."

The two verses that follow are punctuated with regular use of the preposition "for" in English, or γὰρ [*gar*] in Greek. Two uses of "for" in verse 16 and one in verse 17. Meaning that Romans 1:16-17 are modifiers for the preceding context with its main verb. The Greek word for "eager" is the adjective πρόθυμος [*prothumos*] by which Paul described his attitude. Therefore, the only verb in verse 15 is the verb εὐαγγελίζω [*euangelizo*, evangelize]. Romans 1:16-17 are therefore modifying the verb εὐαγγελίζω [*euangelizo*, evangelize], which means that the main verb upon which the content and context of the entire Book of Romans is written is the verb "evangelize"!

Not only that, but, the main verb εὐαγγελίζω [*euangelizo*, evangelize] provides the link between the content of the Book of Romans and the evangelizing in the Book of Acts. The Greek verb εὐαγγελίζω [*euangelizo*, evangelize] is found 15 times in the Book of Acts. It is used 5 times in Acts 8, which describes the ministry of Philip the Evangelist, and it is used 7 times in the context of the ministry of the Apostle Paul. For example, Acts 14:7 is an extremely short verse:

- Acts 14:7, "And there they evangelized [εὐαγγελίζω, *euangelizo*]"

If you wonder what Paul's message was when he was evangelizing in the region of Lycaonia, the simplest exegetical and hermeneutical answer is to look at the Book of Romans! The Book of Romans provides Paul's message of the simple gospel. Paul, who was in prison, was so eager to get to Rome, to evangelize there, that he sent them a letter. And in doing that, he left for all time the core of his message for future generations to read.

So the simplest and easiest way to ascertain if your message conforms to New Testament evangelizing, is to compare it with the Book of Romans. It is for this reason that so many gospel presentations include a type of "Roman Road" outline. Many presentations of the simple gospel include verses like Romans 3:23, Romans 6:23, Romans 5:8, and Romans 10:9-10, 13. And the Lord has used this simple message of the Gospel as described in the Book of Romans to lead many millions of people to salvation in Christ throughout the history of Christ's true church. In fact, if the core message of any church's gospel cannot be found from the Book of Romans, they are not a part of the true church of the Lord Jesus Christ!

So, what is the essential message of the Gospel? It consists of an overview of the Book of Romans. Here is a simple outline of the entire book:

- Man's sinful condition, Rom 1-3
- Justification by faith through the atoning work of Jesus on the cross, Rom 3-5
- Living as slaves of righteousness, Rom 6-8
- Israel's blindness, Rom 9-11
- The word of faith and the hearing of faith, Rom 10
- A life of faith, Rom 12-16

Further, in Romans 10:15, Paul quoted the familiar passage from Isaiah 52:7, which twice used the Greek verb "evangelize":

- Rom 10;15, "And how shall they preach unless they are sent? As it is written: 'How beautiful are the feet of those who evangelize [εὐαγγελίζω, *euangelizo*] peace, Who evangelize [εὐαγγελίζω, *euangelizo*] good!'"

Then towards the end of the Book of Romans, Paul made two statements which relate back to his use of the word "evangelize" in the opening part of the book. First, he repeated the use of the Greek word εὐαγγελίζω [*euangelizo*, evangelize] in Romans 15:20:

- Rom 15:20, "And so I have made it my aim to evangelize [εὐαγγελίζω, *euangelizo*], not where Christ was named, lest I should build on another man's foundation."

Then, as he was wrapping up this important epistle, he included his preaching and his gospel in a doxology:

- Rom 16:25-27, "Now to Him who is able to establish you according to my gospel and the preaching of Jesus Christ, according to the revelation of the mystery kept secret since the world began but now made manifest, and by the prophetic Scriptures made known to all nations, according to the commandment of the everlasting God, for obedience to the faith— to God, alone wise, *be* glory through Jesus Christ forever. Amen."

So, clearly, the primary message of the Gospel for the New Testament evangelist is found in the pages of the Book of Romans.

So, based on the Book of Romans, the personal gospel can be distilled into three main points:

- Sin;
- The work of Jesus Christ;
- Commitment.

Often these points have led to the "Roman Road" gospel plan, for example:

- Mankind's sin problem, Rom 3:9, 19-20, 23
- Righteousness available by faith, Rom 1:16-17; 3:21-24
- Justified by the blood of Christ, Rom 3:25-26; 5:8-9
- God's only condition for salvation, Rom 10:9-10, 13

This provides a complete presentation of the simple gospel.

The evangelist should remember the main elements of the gospel every time he preaches: sin, the work of Christ, and commitment. All three are vital and important. Sin cannot be overlooked, for it is because of sin that the wrath of God is revealed from heaven (Rom 1:18). In fact, preaching sin and God's judgment was very important to revivalist clergyman Devereux Jarrett, who preached in the State of Virginia beginning in 1773:

> "I endeavor to expose, in the most alarming colors, the guilt of sin, the entire depravity of human nature—the awful danger mankind are in by nature and practice—the tremendous curse to which they are obnoxious, and their utter inability to evade the sentence of the law and the strokes of divine justice by their own power, merit, or good works."[3]

Likewise, Jonathan Edward's 1741 sermon, "Sinners in the Hands of an Angry God," focused on man's depravity and God's judgment:

> "I have chosen for my text, **their foot shall slide in due time** [Deut 32:35], seems to imply the following things, relating to the

---

[3] W. M. Geweher, *The Great Awakening in Virginia* (Durham, NC: Duke University, 1930), 139; quoted in W. L. Muncy, Jr., *Evangelism in the United States* (Kansas City, KS: Central Seminary, 1945), 53-54.

punishment and destruction to which these wicked Israelites were exposed…"[4]

Edwards also focused on God's impending judgment:

"There is nothing that keeps wicked men at any one moment out of hell, but the mere pleasure of God…

"So that, thus it is that natural men are held in the hand of God, over the pit of hell; they have deserved the fiery pit, and are already sentenced to it; and God is dreadfully provoked, his anger is as great towards them as to those that are actually suffering the executions of the fierceness of his wrath in hell, and they have done nothing in the least to appease or abate that anger, neither is God in the least bound by any promise to hold them up one moment; the devil is waiting for them, hell is gaping for them, the flames gather and flash about them, and would fain lay hold on them, and swallow them up; the fire pent up in their own hearts is struggling to break out: and they have no interest in any Mediator, there are no means within reach that can be any security to them. In short, they have no refuge, nothing to take hold of; all that preserves them every moment is the mere arbitrary will, and uncovenanted, unobliged forbearance of an incensed God."[5]

Edwards moved from speaking of the Israelites to mankind in his natural state. Then he changed to second person, addressing his audience as "You":

"The use of this awful subject may be for awakening unconverted persons in this congregation. This that you have heard is the case of every one of you that are out of Christ.—That world of misery, that lake of burning brimstone, is extended abroad under you. There is the dreadful pit of the glowing flames of the wrath of God; there is hell's wide gaping mouth open; and you have nothing to stand upon, nor any thing to take hold of; there is nothing between you and hell but the air; it is only the power and mere pleasure of God that holds you up. …

---

[4] Jonathan Edwards, "Sinners in the Hands of an Angry God"; available at: http://www.ccel.org/ccel/ edwards/sermons.sinners.html (online); accessed: 29 June 2012; Internet.

[5]Ibid.

"Your wickedness makes you as it were heavy as lead, and to tend downwards with great weight and pressure towards hell..."[6]

Edwards then addressed their unregenerate state:

"Consider this, you that are here present, that yet remain in an unregenerate state. That God will execute the fierceness of his anger, implies, that he will inflict wrath without any pity..."[7]

Finally, Edwards moved to their need for conversion:

"Thus it will be with you that are in an unconverted state, if you continue in it; the infinite might, and majesty, and terribleness of the omnipotent God shall be magnified upon you, in the ineffable strength of your torments. ...

"Therefore, let every one that is out of Christ, now awake and fly from the wrath to come. The wrath of Almighty God is now undoubtedly hanging over a great part of this congregation. Let every one fly out of Sodom: 'Haste and escape for your lives, look not behind you, escape to the mountain, lest you be consumed.'"[8]

Evangelist, do not leave sinners in the hands of an angry God, without offering them salvation full and free through the shed blood of Jesus. This powerful sermon greatly used by the Lord to spark revival in the United States did not make much of the work of Christ, but rather it focused on God's omnipotence and judgment in relation to man's sin. The name Jesus is never used, but the word Christ is used 9 times. The word "cross" and the word "blood" (when speaking of Christ) were only used once:

"Many are daily coming from the east, west, north and south; many that were very lately in the same miserable condition that you are in, are now in a happy state, with their hearts filled with love to him who has loved them, and washed them from their sins in his own blood, and rejoicing in hope of the glory of God."[9]

---

[6]Ibid.
[7]Ibid.
[8]Ibid.
[9]Ibid.

While every sermon does not have to focus on every part of the gospel, it is commendable for every part of it to be present in the sermon somewhere.

So according to Luke 24:46-47 and 1 Corinthians 15:3-5 the work of Christ is an important part of the simple gospel. Perhaps the single most important element to the work of Christ is the Substitutionary Atonement. While many verses speak of this important doctrine, 2 Corinthians 5:21 is as clear as any:

- 2 Cor 5:21, "For He made Him who knew no sin *to be* sin for us, that we might become the righteousness of God in Him"

The heart of justification by faith is through the Substitutionary Atonement of Jesus. This great doctrine is also highlighted in Isaiah 53, 1 Peter 2:24, and 1 Peter 3:18.

Following are some points from Spurgeon expounding on the shed blood of Jesus, in an 1858 sermon titled, "The Ark of Safety," from Exodus 12:13:

> "The blood is *once shed* for the remission of sin. The paschal lamb was slain every year, but Christ, once for all, hath put away sin by the offering of Himself. He has said, 'It is finished.' Let that ring in thy ears. . . .
>
> "*The blood* is to save thee, not thy tears; *Christ's death, not thy repentance.* ... Friend, it is not thine experience; it is the blood. God did not say, 'When I see your experience,' but, 'When I see *the blood of Christ.*' ...
>
> "O sinner, I have not the shadow of a doubt as to whether Christ will save you, *if* you trust in His blood! I know He will. I am certain His blood can save; and I beg you, in Christ's name, believe it; believe that the blood is *sure* to cleanse, not only that *it may* cleanse, but that *it must* cleanse. If we have that blood upon us we must be saved, or else we are to suppose a God unfaithful. ...
>
> "Sinner, I have a word from the Lord for thee: if you feel your need of a Saviour, that blood is able to save you, and you are bidden simply to trust that blood, and you shall be saved. If you can rely simply on the blood of Christ, that blood is able to save. Leave off

127

doing altogether; get Christ *first*, and then you may do as much as you like. See the Saviour hanging on the cross; turn your eye to Him, and say, 'Lord I trust Thee; I have nothing else to trust to; sink or swim, my Saviour, I trust Thee.' And as surely, sinner, as thou canst put thy trust in Christ, thou art safe. He that believeth shall be saved, be his sins ever so many; he that believeth not shall be damned, be his sins ever so few, and his virtues ever so many. Trust in Jesus *now*, Jesus only."[10]

And here we have the eloquence of Spurgeon, moving from the blood of Christ into the call to commitment, which makes up the third part of the simple gospel, which Jesus called, "Repentance and remission of sins" (Luke 24:47). Spurgeon directly addressed sinners, pleading with them to look to Jesus for forgiveness. That great pulpiteer even recommended to them a prayer, "Lord I trust Thee; I have nothing else to trust to; sink or swim, my Saviour, I trust Thee." He ended his sermon with the admonition, "Trust in Jesus *now*, Jesus only."

So we have the simple gospel: sin, the work of Christ, and commitment. German evangelist August Herman Francke (1663-1727) echoed the importance of sharing this simple of salvation in every message:

> "As far as I am concerned, I must preach that should someone hear me only once before he dies, he will have heard not just a part, but the entire way of salvation and in the proper way for it to take root in his heart."[11]

So how does the Gospel take root in a heart? It takes root when "repentance and remission of sins" are preached in obedience to Jesus' Great Commission in Luke 24.

The evangelist must preach conversion and commitment, a now conversion and urgent commitment:

[10]C. H. Spurgeon, "Salvation and Safety" [a.k.a. "The Blood," 12 Dec 1859] *Royal Dainties*, no. 169 [Minneapolis: Asher Publishing Co., affiliated with The Union Gospel Mission, n.d.], 1, 2, 3, 4; found at http//www.wheaton.edu/bgc/ archives/docs/tract01.html; Internet, accessed 4 January 2001.

[11]Paulus Scharpff, *History of Evangelism: Three Hundred Years of Evangelism in Germany, Great Britain, and the Unites States of America.* Helga Bender Henry, trans. (Grand Rapids: Eerdmans, 1964, 1966), 46.

- Heb 4:7, "Today, if you will hear His voice, Do not harden your hearts."
- 2 Cor 6:2, "Behold, now *is* the accepted time; behold, now *is* the day of salvation"

And exactly to what kind of commitment does the evangelist call sinners? To that of the new birth, "You must be born again":

- John 3:7, "Do not marvel that I said to you, 'You must be born again.'"
- Rom 10:9-10, 13, "that if you confess with your mouth the Lord Jesus and believe in your heart that God has raised Him from the dead, you will be saved. For with the heart one believes unto righteousness, and with the mouth confession is made unto salvation. ... For 'whoever calls on the name of the LORD shall be saved.'"

After preaching sin, after preaching the death of Jesus for sin, and his resurrection power over sin, death, and hell, give the sinner hope by telling him how to receive the forgiveness of sins through Jesus.

As we preach this simple gospel message, the Lord comes near to all who hear (Luke 10:10-11), and we pray that they listen to what they hear:

- Isa 55:6-7, "Seek the LORD while He may be found, Call upon Him while He is near. Let the wicked forsake his way, And the unrighteous man his thoughts; Let him return to the LORD, And He will have mercy on him; And to our God, For He will abundantly pardon."

CHAPTER TEN

THE EVANGELIST AND GOD'S INVITATION

"Anyway you look at it, any way you study it, you will come to the definite conclusion that, granted the invitation is given courteously, as spiritually as possible, the only one who can logically object to it is the prince of Hell."

Hyman Appelman

Perhaps even more controversial than the Sinner's Prayer is the giving of an invitation following a presentation of the gospel. [1] Therefore, seeking to leave aside emotive language and predetermined conclusions, it is our desire in this chapter to: (1) show from the Bible the necessity and urgency of giving invitations, and (2) provide suggestions on giving effective invitations.

The very first words out of God's mouth after the fall of man were in the form of a question to Adam: "Where are you?" (Gen 2:9). All the way through the pages of the Bible we find God calling out to people, and we find their varying responses. Then in the last chapter of Revelation we read the last invitation found in the Bible and inspired by the Holy Spirit:

> "And the Spirit and the bride say, 'Come!' And let him who hears say, 'Come!' And let him who thirsts come. Whoever desires, let him take the water of life freely" (Rev 22:17).

God spoke to Abraham, commanding him to "Get out of his country." He called on him to go "to the land which I will show you"

---

[1] The authors recommend consideration of the invitation used by French Reformed Desert Church preacher Claude Brousson from 1689 to his martyrdom in 1698; available at: http://www.evangelismunlimited.com/invitation.php (online); accessed 24 July 2012; Internet.

(Gen 12:1). God called out to Abraham, invited him to do something, and voiced a blessing to Abraham if he did so. The blessing of Abraham and everything that followed in Salvation History was based on Abraham's positive response to God's invitation. And Abraham obeyed.

Later, in Genesis 15:6, we read that "Abraham believed in the LORD, and He accounted it to him for righteousness." The faith of Abraham certainly was not founded upon a creed, nor upon dialectical speculation on the existence of God. Rather, Abraham believed "the word of the Lord" (Gen 15:4) and acted upon it, just as he had after the Genesis 12 invitation of God. Abraham had an active faith, based upon the very words of the living God.

Sometime later God spoke in the ears of a young man named Samuel. God had not forgotten the dedication of his godly mother, and he had a special task for Samuel. Samuel heard the voice of God, "Samuel." Again and again he heard the voice, until Eli told Samuel to say, "Speak, Lord, for your servant hears" (1 Sam 3:9). Samuel obeyed, praying using the very words as Eli had directed him. God then shared a message of judgment upon the house of Eli:

> "Then Eli called Samuel and said, 'Samuel, my son!' And he answered, 'Here I am.' And he said, 'What *is* the word that *the* LORD spoke to you? Please do not hide *it* from me. God do so to you, and more also, if you hide anything from me of all the things that He said to you.' Then Samuel told him everything, and hid nothing from him. And he said, 'It *is* the LORD. Let Him do what seems good to Him'" (1 Sam 3:16-18).

Samuel told Eli everything, and Eli agreed that the judgment communicated by Samuel was from the Lord. In doing so, Eli confirmed that God does speak to others through His messengers. Yet, while Eli was ready to call a greater curse upon Samuel if he did not declare everything to him, he was not willing to lift a finger to act upon the warning of God. He did not heed the warning, nor did it move him to any action. His was a fatalistic attitude towards God's warning through Samuel. Eli chose spiritual laziness instead of responding in the obedience of faith.

Time and time again God spoke to his people, and time and time again they did not respond. God even spoke to foreign people, some of whom responded, but others did not. Jeremiah summarized God's indictment against His people:

> "'And now, because you have done all these works,' says the LORD, 'and I spoke to you, rising up early and speaking, but you did not hear, and I called you, but you did not answer, therefore I will do to the house which is called by My name, in which you trust, and to this place which I gave to you and your fathers, as I have done to Shiloh'" (Jer 7:13-14).

> "Since the day that your fathers came out of the land of Egypt until this day, I have even sent to you all My servants the prophets, daily rising up early and sending *them.* Yet they did not obey Me or incline their ear, but stiffened their neck. They did worse than their fathers" (Jer 7:25-26).

Yes, God's way of warning His people is often through messengers. It is through His messengers that God moves His people to obedience and action. Yet far too often, God's people turn a deaf ear to the warning from His servants:

> "For the time will come when they will not endure sound doctrine, but according to their own desires, *because* they have itching ears, they will heap up for themselves teachers; and they will turn *their* ears away from the truth, and be turned aside to fables. But you be watchful in all things, endure afflictions, do the work of an evangelist, fulfill your ministry" (2 Tim 4:3-5).

Isn't it interesting that, in the same passage where we read of God's people having itching ears for fables, we also read the command to "Do the work of an evangelist." It is not mere coincidence—it is context! Directly because churches are dying and because God's people are hard of hearing, that's why evangelists are so desperately needed!

Jesus opened his ministry by responding to the invitation of John the Baptist. Listen to the words of the astonished John the Baptist, when Jesus came to him for baptism:

> "Then Jesus came from Galilee to John at the Jordan to be baptized by him. And John *tried to* prevent Him, saying, 'I need to be baptized by You, and are You coming to me?' But Jesus answered and said to him, 'Permit *it to be so* now, for thus it is fitting for us to fulfill all righteousness.' Then he allowed Him. When He had been baptized, Jesus came up immediately from the water; and behold, the heavens were opened to Him, and He saw the Spirit of God descending like a dove and alighting upon Him. And suddenly a voice *came* from heaven, saying, 'This is My beloved Son, in whom I am well pleased'" (Matt 3:13-17).

Imagine the shock of John the Baptist, seeing Jesus the Son of God coming forward to receive baptism for the remission of sins. Yet, responding to John's invitation to come forward inaugurated the ministry of Jesus on earth!

From the early days of His ministry on earth, Jesus also extended invitations, both to individuals and to groups. His most common invitation was, "Follow Me!" We find the invitation, "Follow Me," given to individuals or small groups thirteen times in the Gospels. Jesus also said, "Come and see" to individuals twice. But likewise, Jesus called out to the multitudes:

> "When He had called the people to *Himself*, with His disciples also, He said to them, 'Whoever desires to come after Me, let him deny himself, and take up his cross, and follow Me'" (Mark 8:34).

> "Come to Me, all *you* who labor and are heavy laden, and I will give you rest. Take My yoke upon you and learn from Me, for I am gentle and lowly in heart, and you will find rest for your souls. For My yoke *is* easy and My burden is light" (Matt 11:28-30).

> "But Jesus said, 'Let the little children come to Me, and do not forbid them; for of such is the kingdom of heaven'" (Matt 19:14 and parallels).

> "And Jesus said to them, 'I am the bread of life. He who comes to Me shall never hunger, and he who believes in Me shall never thirst'" (John 6:35).
>
> "On the last day, that great *day* of the feast, Jesus stood and cried out, saying, 'If anyone thirsts, let him come to Me and drink'" (John 7:37).

Throughout His life, Jesus challenged people with their sin and spoke of their relationship with God the Father. He was a living example of being a "fisher of men," just as He had called His disciples to be (Matt 4:19; Mark 4:17). His was a life of "taking men alive" (Luke 5:10).

In fact, Jesus taught His disciples to proclaim the gospel, seeking a response, whether positive or negative. In the sending passages of Matthew 10 and Luke 10, Jesus even taught His disciples to share the gospel to the point of rejection:

> "And whoever will not receive you nor hear your words, when you depart from that house or city, shake off the dust from your feet" (Matt 10:14).
>
> "But whatever city you enter, and they do not receive you, go out into its streets and say, 'The very dust of your city which clings to us we wipe off against you. Nevertheless know this, that the kingdom of God has come near you'" (Luke 10:10-11).

The call to commitment was not neglected in Luke's Great Commission. In Luke 24:46-48 we find not only the message of the gospel from the lips of Jesus, but we also find His desired call to commitment:

> "Then He said to them, 'Thus it is written, and thus it was necessary for the Christ to suffer and to rise from the dead the third day, and that repentance and remission of sins should be preached in His name to all nations, beginning at Jerusalem. You are witnesses of these things'" (Luke 24:46-48).

So the Christian's message of the gospel is to include "repentance and remission of sins." Is this not the means by which the offer of salvation is acquired? It appears to be an echo of the very preaching of Jesus, "Repent and believe the Good News!" (Mark 1:15). Further, in Matthew's Great Commission, Christ called on his followers to win disciples, baptizing "them" (Matt 28:19). Who were they to baptize? Only those who had already become disciples!

So it is clear from the lips of Jesus that the Christian is to call people to repentance and invite them into a right relationship with Christ. And these same examples are found throughout the Book of Acts.

After the great Pentecost sermon, the people cried out to Peter, "Brethren, what shall we do?" Peter answered them, "Repent, and let every one of you be baptized in the name of Jesus Christ for the remission of sins" (Acts 2:38). By repentance they became disciples of Jesus Christ through faith, and by baptism they outwardly professed that commitment before the other disciples and to the world. Was this not the same commitment found in Paul's response to the Philippian jailer, when he cried out, "Sirs, what must I do to be saved?" They told him all that he needed to do to be saved, "Believe on the Lord Jesus Christ, and you will be saved, you and your household" (Acts 16:31). Then through faith alone, he was saved, and that salvation was professed openly through baptism.

And with these and many other examples, we find the New Testament Christian explaining what is needed for salvation to be received. For, just as God uses us to communicate the message of the Gospel, so God also uses us to invite the sinner to receive Christ as Savior.

And now, as we close this section, we return to that great passage in Revelation 22:17:

> "And the Spirit and the bride say, 'Come!'
> "And let him who hears say, 'Come!'
> "And let him who thirsts come.
> "Whoever desires, let him take the water of life freely" (Rev 22:17).

At the close of the New Testament canon, the elder Apostle John extends another invitation. He has already extended various kinds of invitation throughout this epistle. But at the close of his book, the Apostle John reiterates the great invitation of and from God to and through man.

This invitation is the teamwork of the Holy Spirit and the bride of Christ. It is the work of God and the work of man come together. The Holy Spirit speaks through the Word of God to convict men of sin, righteousness, and judgment. And the evangelist, as a representative member of the bride of Christ applies the message of God's Word to the mind, heart, and conscience of the sinner. Just as Nathan the prophet who came to King David in his sinful condition, and brought the judgment of God on him for his sin, saying, "You are the man!" (2 Sam 12:7). The evangelist does not stay in vague abstractions of third person sin. He applies the teachings of the Word of God in the second person, proclaiming the judgment of God on individuals and their sin:

> "This is the critical moment when the one making the appeal moves from first and third person to second person—from 'we' and 'they' to 'you'! And, not second-person plural, but second-person singular. You—*singular*. Here is the moment of challenge, the hinge of the entire gospel appeal."[2]

Likewise, when a man is called on to make the most important decision of his life you must shift to the second personal pronoun "you."

In the second phrase in Revelation 22:17, there is an unusual repetition of the person who says, "Come." This time, John is not speaking in the abstract metaphor of the bride, he speaks of an actual person who hears and harkens to the message. These individuals, designated only as "him who hears," those are people who (1) having heard the message, and (2) having responded positively, (3) are now extending the invitation themselves? They have come full circle.

[2]O.S. Hawkins, *Drawing the Net* (Annuity Board of the SBC, 2002), 30.

These folks represent the evangelized who have now become evangelizers! These are the multitude of the saved ones who are also commanded by Christ to "say, Come!"

While the passage begins in the sense of a general invitation (cf. Col 1:28-29), in the third and fourth phrase it becomes more and more particular. Phrase three begins particularizing with the phrase, "him who thirsts." This is a quote of the great invitation of Isaiah 55:1-2, "Ho! Everyone who thirsts, come to the waters." Jesus repeated this idea when He spoke to the Woman at the Well. He said, "But whoever drinks of the water that I shall give him will never thirst" (John 4:14). It appears that the thirsting in the heart of man comes from the Holy Spirit's wooing them, as they hear Him call to them, "Come!" This "hearing of faith" is given to those who harken to the call, as mentioned in Isaiah 55:2, "Listen carefully to Me." In the third phrase of Rev 22:17, these thirsting ones are also commanded to "Come!"

In the fourth phrase, John writes of God's working through men's desires, by stating, "Whoever desires." This free offer of salvation is extended to all who hear and to all who desire. Every man, woman, boy and girl are bidden to come before it is too late. They are to come publicly and unashamedly. So what is God's invitation from the lips of His evangelists? It is, "Come!" Come to Jesus. Turn from your sin. Turn to God. Come to Him today!

As the evangelist, the pastor, or the Christian considers the weighty responsibility of extending an invitation, it can sometimes become overwhelming. John Bisagno, retired pastor of First Baptist Church, Houston, Texas, wrote, "Extending an invitation is the greatest agony in the ministry."[3] The response of King David to the promise of God is applicable here: "Who am I and what is my house that thou hast brought me this far? … Now what more can David say to You? For You, Lord GOD, know Your servant" (2 Sam 7:18, 20). Certainly, Paul echoed this sentiment of inadequacy in 2 Corinthians 2:15-17:

---

[3]John R. Bisagno, *The Power of Positive Evangelism*, 13.

137

"For we are to God the fragrance of Christ among those who are being saved and among those who are perishing. To the one *we are* the aroma of death *leading* to death, and to the other the aroma of life *leading* to life. And who *is* sufficient for these things? For we are not, as so many, peddling the word of God; but as of sincerity, but as from God, we speak in the sight of God in Christ" (2 Cor 2:15-17).

Paul, understanding the eternal ramifications of the response to his words, wrote, "And who is sufficient for these things?" Dear reader, you may say, "This is too much. How can I expect that God will use the words formed off my tongue to lead people either to eternal life or eternal death?" Truly, it is a solemn truth. But it is so.

Proverbs 18:21 states that death and life are in the power of the tongue. In ourselves we are inadequate for such a weighty task. But it is the work of the Holy Spirit through us. We are pleading, but He is pleading. He is urging, so we are urging. Even now He is working; even now we are working! Truly we are co-laborers with Christ:

"Now then, we are ambassadors for Christ, as though God were pleading through us: we implore *you* on Christ's behalf, be reconciled to God. For He made Him who knew no sin *to be* sin for us, that we might become the righteousness of God in Him. We then, *as* workers together *with Him* also plead with *you* not to receive the grace of God in vain. For He says: 'In an acceptable time I have heard you, And in the day of salvation I have helped you.' Behold, now *is* the accepted time; behold, now *is* the day of salvation. (2 Cor 5:20-6:2).

A man after God's own heart is a man concerned with the salvation of all people. Jesus came to seek and to save that which is lost. Our command is, "As the Father hath sent me even so send I you." Jesus came to save sinners. We are to call men to Jesus so He can save them. We are to call them unashamedly and wholeheartedly. If we are not calling men to come, we are not fulfilling God's call on our lives. The Church has no business going on a sit down strike against Christ's Great Commission!

Because of its special divine nature, the invitation is the most difficult part of any sermon. Pastors have consistently told Keith for over 40 years of evangelism ministry that the most difficult part of the sermon is the invitation. It is at the point of invitation that the audience is left, either as one who listens to a well-played instrument, or as one who will be serious about what they have just heard!

> "Indeed you *are* to them as a very lovely song of one who has a pleasant voice and can play well on an instrument; for they hear your words, but they do not do them. And when this comes to pass—surely it will come—then they will know that a prophet has been among them" (Ezek 33:32-33).

Is there anything that the preacher can do to move his audience from being disengaged spectators to active participants? Here is the sixty-four dollar question.

Paul used all the knowledge that he had of the Old Testament Scriptures combined with all his powers of persuasion to move his audiences, and we ought to do the same:

> "So when they had appointed him a day, many came to him at *his* lodging, to whom he explained and solemnly testified of the kingdom of God, persuading them concerning Jesus from both the Law of Moses and the Prophets, from morning till evening. And some were persuaded by the things which were spoken, and some disbelieved" (Acts 28:23-24).

Notice Luke's double use of the verb "persuade" to describe Paul's last evangelism encounter in the Book of Acts. Just as in Paul's example, the evangelist is to "persuade" his audience concerning Jesus. And this intense and long persuasion of Paul had mixed results: "Some were persuaded by the things which were spoken, and some disbelieved." Notice the importance of "the things which were spoken." Is this not reminiscent of Lydia's conversion: "And the Lord opened her heart to heed the things spoken by Paul" (Acts 16:14).

So then Acts 28:23-24 provides an excellent example of the winnowing fork of the Holy Spirit dividing congregations asunder:

some believe and some choose to disbelieve. And this division took place between them all because Paul was seeking to persuade them!

So, persuasion is not a bad thing. In fact, it is a part of the biblical example for New Testament evangelizing. Are there limits to the use of human persuasion? Yes. Let's remember that New Testament evangelizing conforms to a New Testament ethic ("Let your yes be yes and your no be no"; "Do not lie to one another"; etc.). Nor does God want us to be too flashy with the wisdom of words:

> "For Christ did not send me to baptize, but to preach the gospel, not with wisdom of words, lest the cross of Christ should be made of no effect" (1 Cor 1:17).

There are some ethically-sound principles for preaching God's Word and extending God's invitation. The following are some principles based on the verbs in 2 Timothy 4:2:

> "Preach the word! Be ready in season *and* out of season. Convince, rebuke, exhort, with all longsuffering and teaching" (2 Tim 4:2).

Convince: You must reason with the audience. Use all the powers of persuasion at your disposition, with an understanding of the abilities of your audience to convince them of their need for Jesus.

Rebuke: A loving rebuke from the Lord Jesus will stir the hearts of your audience. Be Scriptural in your rebuke. This word coupled with the idea of doctrine indicates that in rebuking we are to bring proof directly from the Word of God. In rebuking, you may need to be blunt. Rebuking can be direct, but it can also be indirect, by using the example of others. It is at this point that illustrations can be used with power. By the way, proper rebuking is a very serious matter! Your rebuke may save a marriage, stop a crime, and even save a life, especially when men are hearing from God. You can stand in the gap by challenging people to stand for what is right. The word rebuke carries the idea of warning the person whether they take heed or not.[4]

Exhort: The word exhort comes from the Greek word *parakaleo*. The word exhort is a very familiar Greek word for most preachers. It is *"parakaleson." "Parakaleo"* is the root verb that we get the word *parakleton* or *paraclete* from speaking of the Holy Spirit as the one called to our side. Exhort literally means to call someone to stand by you in the truth that you have preached. Thus it refers to "beside-call" or "beside-calling." The Greek word παρακαλέω [*parakaleo*] is used 108 times in the New Testament. It is often translated "exhort," especially in proclamational contexts (cf. Acts 2:40; 14:22; 15:32). It is translated "appeal" in Acts 16:9, "plead" in Acts 16:39, and "entreat" in 2 Corinthians 5:20. On the other hand, it is also translated "encourage" or "comfort" in Acts 16:40; 20:12. According to the 1875 Liddell-Scott lexicon, the primary meaning of παρακαλέω [*parakaleo*] is "to call for one"; hence "to summon," or "to invite." Flowing from these meanings, then, the word began to take on the more abstract meanings of "to call to, call on, exhort," as well as "to demand, require." In its basic meaning, however, the verb παρακαλέω [*parakaleo*] corresponds to the evangelist inviting sinners to his side, so that he can lead them to become Christ-followers. This meaning corresponds with that which took place after Paul's Athenian discourse in Acts 17:

> "And when they heard of the resurrection of the dead, some mocked, while others said, 'We will hear you again on this *matter.*' So Paul departed from among them. However, some men joined him and believed, among them Dionysius the Areopagite, a woman named Damaris, and others with them" (Acts 17:32-34).

This concept of "joining" Paul is actually another interesting verb, meaning "to cleave." It is clear that there was physical proximity involved in these people joining Paul![5]

---

[4]Keith Fordham, "God's Invitation: How to Give an Invitation"; this sermon was first preached at the Alabama Pastor's Conference, then later at the 2002 Georgia Evangelism Conference at First Baptist Church, Jonesboro, Georgia.

[5]The Greek verb for "joining" in Acts 17:34 is κολλάω. This same verb is found of Philip joining the chariot of the Ethiopian Eunuch (Acts 8:29), of Paul seeking to join himself to the

Similarly, Peter began his famous invitation in Acts 2 with a call to repentance and faith (vv. 38-39). Then his invitation changed tones to a more aggressive message in verse 40:

> "And with many other words he testified and exhorted [parakaleo] them, saying, 'Be saved from this perverse generation.' Then those who gladly received his word were baptized; and that day about three thousand souls were added *to them*" (Acts 2:40-41).

After urgently "inviting" (parakaleo) them to save themselves (passive voice) from this perverse generation, 3,000 were identified as having gladly receive his words, and they were all baptized. Surely, Peter's invitation allowed him and the disciples to identify, count, and baptize each individual. They responded to Peter's call to "come beside" him; his was a "beside call"—this is the literal meaning of the Greek word *para-kaleo*.

Similarly and strikingly, note what the new converts did immediately after their conversion. Luke used three specialized verbs to describe their actions.

(1) Luke used the verb ἀκολουθέω (*akoloutheo*, to follow or to continue; 82 NT uses), as found in Acts 13:43:

> "Now when the congregation had broken up, many of the Jews and devout proselytes followed Paul and Barnabas, who, speaking to them, persuaded them to continue in the grace of God."

This exact same verb is used of the disciples following Jesus (Matt 4:20; Mark 1:18; Luke 5:11; etc.). Just as the disciples followed Jesus, so the new converts in Acts were "following" Paul and Barnabas!

(2) In Acts 17:4, an interesting set of verbs is used. First the verb "persuade," which we have already noted, and also the verb "joined." The verb προσκληρόω [*proskleroo*] is used only once in the New Testament, and means "to be attached to, to join." In whatever way

---

disciples in Jerusalem (Acts 9:26), and of Peter explaining how unlawful it was for Jews to join himself to a Gentile (Acts 10:28). In Romans 12:9, Paul uses this word when he wrote, "Cleave to what is good."

they responded to the invitation of Paul, it meant that they actively sought him out and became attached to him.

(3) The third verb has already been noted above, it is found in Acts 17:34. It means "to cleave." The verb is κολλάω [*kollao*]. It is very interesting to see the variety of verbs that Luke used to describe the actions after Paul's invitation: follow, join, and cleave to. Clearly, these people responded positively to Paul's call to "come beside" him!

Further, consider, the two Greek forms normally translated "Follow Me." When Jesus called His first disciples, it was literally to "Come after him" (Δεῦτε ὀπίσω μου, *deute opiso mou*; Matt 4:19; Mark 1:17). Physical movement was implied in this word picture. In all the other calls of Christ translated "Follow me," another Greek verb is used (ἀκολουθέω, *akoloutheo*). Thus, in both cases, emphatic or not, the New Testament was not adverse to the need for physical movement on the part of responsive persons!

So the evangelist is to convince, rebuke, and exhort, and to do so with all longsuffering and doctrine. As he does so, some will respond with an amazing level of commitment and stand beside the evangelist. Therefore, it is clear that a part of the evangelist's office includes inviting sinners to repentance, and inviting them to come alongside. Likewise the evangelist's office includes inviting believers to rededication, inviting them to come alongside. And this is to be done with patience, kindness, and sound doctrine.

Often, inviting to come alongside is called an "invitation." Rather than being a "system,"[6] the invitation is an opportunity for true teaching, encouragement, and exhortation to take place. And, once a person comes forward, this exhortation can be done one-on-one. The evangelist, the pastor, or a trained counselor can meet the inquirer, and lovingly assist them in their spiritual needs and pray for them.

---

[6] A truly impersonal "system" of salvation is infant baptism. The person being "ministered to" has no idea what is happening. It is ritualistic and robotic. Dealing one-on-one with a convicted soul who has responded to an invitation is a completely different matter.

Bisagno, for his part, encouraged pastors, preachers, and evangelists to follow eleven suggestions for extending invitations. These eleven points come from his book *The Power of Positive Evangelism*:[7]

1. Give the invitation authoritatively. [It is a privilege to extend the invitation of the King of Kings, so do it with authority].
2. Be specific. Never assume that your audience knows what you want them to do.
3. Give it urgently—Never ask them to think it over. ... it is always now, now, now!
4. Get into the invitation.
5. Give the invitation positively.
6. Give the invitation prayerfully.
7. Give it proudly.
8. Don't be afraid to give long invitations.
9. Give a good rededication invitation.
10. Deal properly with those who come.
11. Make much of their decision.

Bisagno reminded his readers that giving an invitation is a God-given gift, and one that will not be learned overnight. For this reason, he provided these suggestions as guidelines both as a reminder to the seasoned preacher, as well as encouragement to those starting out in the preaching ministry.

When the preacher comes to the invitation, this is where he opens his heart to his audience. All the mental efforts by which he has opened the Word of God either collude or collide at the invitation, as he shares his heart's desire for his audience. He feels alone, exposed. He may feel over-prepared or under-prepared; it's hard to find a good balance. He either retreats in his mind from the sea of faces before him, or feels empowered from above as his words sink deeply into every listening heart. Sometimes he may feel the electricity of the Holy Spirit—God gives him one powerful exhortation after another! At other times he may feel woefully

[7]Bisagno, *The Power of Positive Evangelism*, 14-25.

inadequate. Whatever the case, dear brother, press on, and don't give up. God will use you as you as you obey His command and say, "Come! … Come! … Come!"

CHAPTER ELEVEN

REVIVAL MUSIC

"Worship is when holiness and salvation kiss,
Resulting in a lifelong love affair to be shared with a lost and needy world."

Rick Stone

"Now therefore, write down this song for yourselves, and teach it to the
children of Israel; put it in their mouths, that this song may be a witness for
Me against the children of Israel"

Deut 31:19

The musician places words in people's hearts, and the song leader places words on people's lips. These are two powerful instruments. Personally, I (Tom) battle secular songs that I heard in my youth. Words were placed in my heart and on my lips that I do not prefer to remember. Words like "I shot the sheriff" are lodged somewhere in the recesses of my mind, only to surface at odd times. It is far preferable to have other words in our minds, such as "All for Jesus, All for Jesus" or "Marvelous Grace of Our Loving Lord." Some of us may have choruses come to mind like, "Take me into the holy of holies" or "He is jealous for me, loves like a hurricane, I am a tree...."

God, knowing the power of words put to music directed Moses to put perhaps the most important words in Deuteronomy into music. Deuteronomy 32 finds its importance in the fact that it teaches the need for the revival of the people of God throughout the centuries. The application is both to the Old Covenant as well as the New Covenant. God in His mercy declared to Moses:

> "Behold, you will rest with your fathers; and this people will rise and play the harlot with the gods of the foreigners of the land, where they go *to be* among them, and they will forsake Me and break My covenant which I have made with them (Deut 31:16)

God prophesied to and through Moses that the people of God would violate the covenant to which, they verbally agreed to, with God. So God gave an unusual remedy—a song: the Song of Moses!

It just so happens that from this same Psalm of Moses, Jonathan Edwards preached a sermon which is often considered to have been the spark of the First Great Awakening, "Sinners in the Hands of an Angry God." He preached this sermon from Deuteronomy 32:35:

"Vengeance is Mine, and recompense;
"Their foot shall slip in *due* time;
"For the day of their calamity *is* at hand,
"And the things to come hasten upon them" (Deut 32:35).

"Their" in this verse refers to the people of God! Notice the hastening calamity upon the people of God prophesied by God through Moses. This is reminiscent of the preaching of Jesus saying that the "Rulership of God is at hand." The summary of the preaching of Jesus was that God would exercise His right to rule and exact judgment.

So Moses took Deuteronomy 32, put into a song, and placed it in the mouths of God's people. Now, why did God ask Moses to write a song? He did this so that His people would repent and return to Him:

> "Then it shall be, when many evils and troubles have come upon them, that this song will testify against them as a witness; for it will not be forgotten in the mouths of their descendants" (Deut 31:21).

God's specific desire for the Song of Moses was to be a wake-up call for His erring people. Interestingly, in Tom's 12 years of Bible education, never in any class, Old Testament or other, did he ever remember looking at Deuteronomy 32—other than one history professor who mentioned Deut 32:7 in passing. Now, by the grace of God, Tom has a B.A. in Bible, a Master of Divinity, and a Ph.D. in evangelism:

> "Then My anger shall be aroused against them in that day, and I will forsake them, and I will hide My face from them, and they shall be devoured. And many evils and troubles shall befall them, so that they will say in that day, 'Have not these evils come upon us because our God *is* not among us?'" (Deut 31:17).

Yes, God wanted the revival of the people. Similarly, in the New Testament, God prophesied through Paul that wolves would come into the church:

> "For I know this, that after my departure savage wolves will come in among you, not sparing the flock. Also from among yourselves men will rise up, speaking perverse things, to draw away the disciples after themselves" (Acts 20:29-30).

Likewise, Paul prophesied that God's people would seek out false teachers to tickle their ears:

> "For the time will come when they will not endure sound doctrine, but according to their own desires, *because* they have itching ears, they will heap up for themselves teachers; and they will turn *their* ears away from the truth, and be turned aside to fables" (2 Tim 4:3-4).

Paul's remedy was for Timothy to "Do the work of an Evangelist." God's remedy for this problem was given in Deuteronomy 31-32. And through this Song of Moses, the godly musician is given his marching orders to keep the fires of revival burning in the church of God.

Music is a powerful weapon, and when God specifically asks that it be used, we should use it! In the New Testament one of the admonitions related to music is found in Colossians 3:16. In this verse two verbs are joined together with an adverb:

"Let the word of Christ dwell in you richly in all wisdom, teaching and admonishing one another in psalms and hymns and spiritual songs, singing with grace in your hearts to the Lord" (Col 3:16).

The two verbs are teaching and admonishing. The first verb is quite clear. However, the second verb needs some introduction. The verb is translated "admonishing" or "exhorting." However, it is not the same verb that we saw for "exhorting" in Chapter Ten (παρακαλέω or *parakaleo*). It is a lesser used verb which comes from the Greek root word for "mind" (νουθετέω or *noutheteo*). Perhaps one may consider a mother who tells her child, "Now mind your manners." She is exhorting her child to think about his or her behavior, and to consider the consequences of that behavior. This warning is also a part of the role of music in the life of the New Testament church. Paul's verbs are therefore not too far afield from the message of Deuteronomy 31 and 32!

Next is the adverb "one another." This adverb is used 62 times in the New Testament to describe life in the New Testament church. For example, "Love one another" is found 12 times in the New Testament. Likewise, Jesus said that His exhortation was a "new commandment." Whereas "loving" was already commanded in the Old Testament; it appears that the "one another" is the new part of the equation. The body of Christ did not exist until Pentecost Sunday. In the New Testament church, therefore, music is not only to teach, but it is also to admonish the people of God.

Revival music, however, focuses on several main points that differ from general "praise and worship." These points are developed in Deuteronomy 32. Revival music focuses on:

- The sin and rebellion of God's people;
- The salvation of God, which from a New Testament perspective is the cross of Christ (1 Cor 2:2);
- The urgency of making things right with God "right now."

Thus revival music also focuses on need for, urgency of, and blessings of a decision for Christ.

In bridging the distinctions between Old Testament worship and New Testament worship, let us consider the "Songs of Heaven" in Revelation 4 and 5. In Revelation 4 the emphasis is upon God, His creative authority and His sovereignty. However, an important change takes place after the exalted Lamb of God is introduced at the beginning of chapter 5. In Revelation 5 the emphasis of the songs change and are now focused on the Lamb of God and His crucifixion! It is actually a very interesting shift, which also relates to the shift from the Psalter, which focused only very slightly on the Lamb (e.g. Psa 22 and 110),as compared to the focus of the New Testament church, which now ought to worship and praise both He who sits on the throne and the Lamb that was slain. This New Testament focus is the reason that much of our hymnody, and particularly our revival songs, focus on Jesus and His work.

Why then is Deuteronomy 32 the most important chapter in the Book of Deuteronomy? First, this chapter gives God's promised song which will convict the people of their rebellion and restore them to a right relationship with him (revival). Further, Deuteronomy 32 provides the hermeneutical or interpretive grid for the five books of Moses (which are foundational to understanding the entire Old Testament). Stated another way, this chapter gives the Bible reader the things to look for when reading the five books of Moses (in theology this is also called the Central Interpretive Motif—CIM). We ignore this CIM to our spiritual detriment.

So, revival is a must, all the way back to the Book of Deuteronomy, and music is front and central in revival!

In a chapel service at Wheaton College in 1950, God used the Second verse of the hymn, "If I Gain the World but Lose the Savior" to pour revival down upon those in attendance. Tom's mother recalled specifically that Verse 2 struck the chapel like lightning:

> Had I wealth and love in fullest measure,
> And a name revered both far and near,
> Yet no hope beyond, no harbor waiting,
> Where my storm-tossed vessel I could steer;

If I gained the world, but lost the Savior,
Who endured the cross and died for me,
Could then all the world afford a refuge,
Whither, in my anguish, I might flee?[1]

This move of God went on for weeks, as Verse 2 brought people to tears of brokenness and commitment to the Savior. The overflow of this move of God is only now waning as those impacted move on to their reward in heaven. Hundreds of these students went into missionary service. Many went to the far reaches of the world, all because of God's Spirit coming down upon Verse 2 of a hymn originally written in Swedish by Anna Ölander and translated into English by some unknown individual.

Music is effective in bringing people to Christ. Music can have a powerful impact for edification and evangelism. Where music in the New Testament appears primarily to have a discipleship or edification function, there are several times in the Old Testament where God-honoring music was used for the lost and wayward. Saul, for example, called on David when he was being harassed by a demon. In this case, David would play and sing one of his psalms, and the demon would cease disturbing Saul:

> "And so it was, whenever the spirit from God was upon Saul, that David would take a harp and play *it* with his hand. Then Saul would become refreshed and well, and the distressing spirit would depart from him (1 Sam 16:23).

Later, Psalm 137 described the children of Israel in captivity, due to their wickedness and sin, and their captors asking of them to sing a song of Zion. Here is an interesting case where foreigners to God's grace were requesting to hear God-exalting music:

> "By the rivers of Babylon,
> "There we sat down, yea, we wept

---

[1] "If I Gained the World But Lost the Savior"; available at: Source: http://www.hymnal.net/hymn.php /h/1079#ixzz20N2DsxmN (online); accessed 11 July 2012; Internet.

"When we remembered Zion.

"We hung our harps

"Upon the willows in the midst of it.

"For there those who carried us away captive asked of us a song,

"And those who plundered us *requested* mirth,

"*Saying*, 'Sing us *one* of the songs of Zion!'

"How shall we sing the LORD's song

"In a foreign land?

"If I forget you, O Jerusalem,

"Let my right hand forget *its skill*!

"If I do not remember you,

"Let my tongue cling to the roof of my mouth—

"If I do not exalt Jerusalem

"Above my chief joy" (Psalm 137:1-6).

So then, it appears that Christian music is not only for Christian audiences. God-honoring Christian music is also desired by lost people, because they hear of the hope and confidence of God's people in the salvation of the Lord. Lost people sense the joy of the Lord—even if only but for a fleeting moment! They consider that there is a God who can actually save them!

Yes, music is a powerful tool to move in the heart of man. Just as it was powerful enough from the fingers and voice of David to exorcize demons from distressing King Saul, the Holy Spirit of God can anoint Scripture-bathed, God-honoring music to move in the hearts of unsaved people, preparing them to hear the Gospel of Christ, and then move on them to repent of their sins and believe in the Good News. He has done so in the past, and He can and will do so in the future!

"'I've got a song that's going to live!' declared Charles Gabriel, a Gospel song writer, to a Chicago publisher. The two men were bicycle riding, during the summer of 1900. The song to which Gabriel referred was *Oh That Will Be Glory,* or as it is best known, *The Glory Song.*

"He was right. It enjoyed a remarkable popularity, but the author received only ten dollars for all the publishing rights to his splendid song.

"Perhaps the *Glory Song* would not have been nearly so well-known had it not been for Charles M. Alexander, the Gospel singer, who traveled all over the English speaking world, singing it.

"'I remember quite well the first time I saw this song in looking over a new songbook,' said Alexander. 'I just glanced at it, and then said to myself, "That man has wasted a page, for I do not believe that song will be sung much.'"

"Alexander heard the song sung in a large Sunday School convention several months later by the audience, and it had the same effect on him it has on all who hear this remarkable hymn.

"'It took such a hold of me that I could think of nothing else for days thereafter. I got my friends to sing it. Then I began to teach it to large audiences, and soon whole towns were ringing with the melody.'

"The singer went to Australia on a tour. Everywhere he sang the *Glory Song,* it took the audience by storm. He had leaflets with the *Glory Song* printed on them and an invitation to the meetings. These were scattered far and wide.

"The story is told of a lady who, after returning home from the service, had a pair of shoes which needed mending. She sent them to the shoemaker, but before wrapping the paper around them, she slipped in a copy of the *Glory Song.*

"When she returned for the shoes next day, the man was nailing a new sole on a shoe before him, and there were tears in his eyes.

"'What is the matter?' the woman asked.

"'That *Glory Song* you put into the bundle. Last night my family and I gathered around the old organ while we sang it. We saw the invitation to hear Torrey and Alexander at the Town Hall, and I went last night. I sent my wife and children this afternoon, and I am praying that God will save them. And God did save them.' The next night the whole family publicly confessed their acceptance of Jesus Christ."[2]

This marvelous song was "Oh, That Will Be Glory," by Charles H. Gabriel. Here is the refrain of that song:

"Oh, that will be glory for me,
"Glory for me, glory for me,

---

[2]Helen C. Alexander and J. Kennedy Maclean, *Charles M. Alexander: A Romance of Song and Soul Winning* (Murfreesboro, TN: Sword of the Lord, 1995), 65-66.

"When by His grace I shall look on His face,
"That will be glory, be glory for me."

The travel and work of this song provides a brief taste of how songs make their way into contemporary usage. It was in fact travelling Evangelists, Camp Meetings, itinerant Music Evangelists, and circuit riders who brought songs from one area to another. Long before the radio waves or I-Pods were disseminating Christian music, travelling Evangelists and their Music Evangelists were leading the charge. Ira Sankey travelled with Evangelist D. L. Moody, Charles Alexander traveled with R. A. Torrey, William Ramsey travelled with Mordecai Ham, and George Beverly Shea and Cliff Barrows travelled with Billy Graham. Among many others, Evangelist John Welsey's brother, Charles, was a prolific hymn writer. All of these men left a legacy of music wherever they went. And it was amazingly the spiritual depth, sing-ability, and adaptability of hymns that had long-standing impact.

In 1952, in the earlier years of his ministry, Evangelist Billy Graham explained the simple role of hymns in his early evangelistic campaigns:

"We allow no instruments in our service except the organ and the piano, except that once in a while Cliff Barrows will bring his trombone. Many of our evangelistic services in America have been more or less a programme of all sorts of music, and have become a musical event. We don't do that. We have Beverley Shea to sing, and he and the choir choose songs in which they bring a message to the people, to prepare them spiritually. Cliff Barrows has also cut out all choruses. We do not sing choruses—not because we do not like choruses or because we don't believe in choruses, but because the pendulum in America has swung so far to this type of business, that we decided to swing it back the other way. And the shock of having none of this is attracting large numbers of people. And so we are singing nothing but the old hymns."[3]

---

[3]Billy Graham, "The Work of an Evangelist," in *Introducing Billy Graham: The Work of an Evangelist—An Address Given at the Assembly Hall of the Church House, Westminster, on*

The emphasis was not on the musician, or even on the music, but on the preparation of the audience to hear the gospel.

The actual marriage of Evangelical revival and the dissemination of songs goes back long before the United States was colonized by the British. Whenever God saves people, He puts a song in their heart. In 1529 an Anabaptist songwriter was arrested and burned alive in Augsburg, Germany.[4] In 1558, an Anabaptist singer[5] was also arrested and burned alive in Kortrijck, Flanders. The same was also true of the Geneva Reformation. Bible colporteurs from Geneva were arrested and burned alive for illegally selling Bibles and Geneva Psalters deep in the heart of Roman Catholic France and Belgium.[6] God-exalting music was important as people were saved and they treasured God's Word in their hearts, passing on God's blessing in song.

Paulus Scharpff explained the role of music beginning with the Eighteenth Century revivals in Germany:

"Music, especially the hymn, also greatly served the cause of evangelism. Every revival, it seems, brings to light new songs

---

20th March, 1952, Prologue and Epilogue by Frank Colquhoun (London: World's Evangelical Alliance, 1953), 22.

[4] [In 1529] "Anabaptist hymn writer Hans [John] Hut was tortured and burned in Augsburg, after his torture and death, he was officially condemned to death by fire" (expanded from Thomas P. Johnston, *Evangelism in the Western Church* [Liberty, MO: Evangelism Unlimited, 2011], 67); "This Jon Hut composed a hymn of thanksgiving, which we sing at the memorial or supper of the Lord; besides this he composed one or two other hymns" (Thieleman J. van Braght, *The Bloody Theater or Martyrs Mirror of the Defenseless Christians Who Baptized Only Upon the Confession of Faith, and Who Suffered and Died for the Testimony of Jesus, Their Savior, From the Time of Christ to the Year A.D. 1660*, trans from the Dutch by Joseph Sohm, 2nd English edition [1660; 1837; 1886; Scottdale, PA: Herald Press, 2007], 433).

[5] [In 1558] "At Kortrijck, Flanders: A. van Tomme (the singer) burned" (Johnston, *Evangelism in the Western Church*, 94; cited from Thieleman J. van Braght, *The Bloody Theater or Martyrs Mirror*, 582).

[6] For example, in 1554, T. Calbergue was burned alive in Tournay [in today's Belguim] for owning a Geneva songbook, and for writing spiritual songs (Jean Crespin, *Histoire des vrais tesmoins de la verite de l'evangile, qui de leur sang l'ont signée, depuis Jean Hus iusques autemps present* [*History of the True Witnesses to the Truth of the Gospel, Who with Their Blood Signed, from John Hus to the Present Time*] (Geneva: Crespin, 1570; Liège: Centre nationale de recherches d'histoire religieuse, 1964), 290 v-291 v; translation mine). On April 30, 1556, François de Mauny, Archbishop of Bordeaux, officially prohibited the singing of the Psalms at home, church, or in the streets, nor sale or owning of Psalms or New Testaments in French (ibid., 437).

inasmuch as revival leads people to spiritual experiences which the literary gifted are moved to express in some exalted fashion. Thus the pietistic movement brought forth a surprising wealth of hymns. The subjective appropriation of objective, redemptive truths gave rise to salvation songs that expressed the personal experiences of repentance and forgiveness, of faith and assurance. In short, songs of testimony, songs of praise for God's love, and songs of prayer and petition came into being."[7]

May this God-blessed marriage of revival and song continue!

But, how can song be appropriately used in the revival service? While this topic could be and has been the subject of entire books, we will glean truths from Keith Fordham's "Revival Evangelism Music" and John Bisagno's chapter "Music," in his *The Power of Positive Evangelism*. Following are seven observations, and some concluding recommendations.

1. The reverent preparation of the song leader as the master of ceremonies is equally important as that of the preacher.

The song leader is not to preach, nor ought he to take much time in introducing each song. He is to allow the preaching to be the role of the preacher. His place is to wisely and humbly lead the audience into the presence of the Most High God and to the foot of the cross. If they are down, he needs to encourage them. If they are sleepy, he needs to wake them up. If they are rushed and anxious, he is to bring them calm.

The love of God and the grace of God will either flow from his face, his words, and his actions, or they will not. Therefore, it is imperative that he be a man of unusual spiritual stature, with a heart for the lost. For a song leader to be effective in evangelism, he must be a regular personal soul winner.

---

[7]Paulus Scharpff, *History of Evangelism*, 53. This quote is taken from Scharpff's Chapter III, "Evangelistic Movements in the Eighteenth Century," Section A, "Germany," Subsection 8, "Evangelism through Religious Literature and Song."

The song leader is the only person within a large meeting that places words on the lips of the people (cf. Deut 31:19), he ought to take special heed which words he places on their lips!

2. While the song leader or Music Evangelist is extremely important, the focus of the evangelistic or revival service must remain on the Evangelist:.

Because the Evangelist is the chief spokesperson, just like Paul was called Hermes, "because he was the chief speaker" (Acts 14:12), so the attention of the meeting should be made to focus on the Evangelist, his preaching, and God's invitation. It will be the Evangelist that will bring the direct message of the gospel and call people to immediate repentance and faith. Although music ought to compliment the message, in the evangelistic meeting, everything the Music Evangelist does should prepare the people to hear the word of Christ.

3. Evangelistic music should always focus on Jesus and His grace and mercy as demonstrated on the cross.

Further, the attention of the people should not be on the song leader, nor on the musicians, but on the Lord Jesus. As was mentioned above, the focus of the "Songs of Heaven" in Revelation 5 should be emulated in the revival services: the Lamb that was slain; the redemption that He purchased; His worthiness; that which He did for us; etc. The revival service is not a place to sing "Faith or Our Fathers" or "All Creatures of Our God and King." The Stamps Quartet Music Company had it right in their *Soul-Winning Revival Songs*:

- #1, "I Will Sing the Wondrous Story";
- #11, "Praise him, Praise Him";
- #12, "When We All Get to Heaven";
- #16, "Are You Washed in the Bloods?";
- #17, "Kneel at the Cross";
- #25, "Lily of the Valley";

- #26, "I Love to Tell the Story";
- #28, "Jesus Saves";
- #29, "Tell Me the Story of Jesus."[8]

And this is only the beginning of this small song book. Oh! That all the songs in a revival reflect Paul's statement in 1 Cor 2:2, "For I determined not to know anything among you except Jesus Christ and Him crucified."

4. The style of revival music should be consistent with the anticipated target audience:

The style of music ought not to be a distraction. Again, all important is the heart of the Music Evangelist. If he is truly desirous of focusing on Jesus, this will come out in his music repertoire and in his leading. The style of music ought not draw the people's attention away from the cross, nor seek to wow or shock them so that they say, "Who is this singer?" but rather, "Who is this Savior?" This role was exemplified by John the Baptist, who said of Jesus, "He must increase, but I must decrease" (John 3:30).

Rick Stone wrote of this selfless focus on the harvest worship leader:

"My passion is to encourage God's musicians to genuinely love Jesus, allowing the Holy Spirit to control their lives and to live in obedience to the Word of God. I love Spirit-filled singing, but I am more interested in the singer. I am blessed by Christ honoring music. But my concern is the musician you see. If the musician is not authentic, the music is 'sounding brass and tinkling symbols.' God is much more interested in the condition of the heart; Than HE is in the sound of the voice! Although God loves our music, HE loves us more."[9]

---

[8] *Soul-Winning Revival Songs*, "Shape Notes Only" (Dallas, TX: Stamps Quartet Music Company, n.d.).

[9] Keith Fordham, "Revival Evangelism Music." Unpublished manuscript.

5. Revival music should follow patterns to properly prepare the audience to hear God's message:

Historically, churches which have focused on the Word of God preached, have used music as a preparation for coming into the presence of God. Therefore, it may be expedient for the musician to consider the Old Testament metaphor that he is like a guide, leading his audience to the Temple of God and into the Holy of Holies.

- Praise: Praise in the streets as the people make their way to the Temple;
- Confession: Confession and contrition as they pass through the outer courts, where the large sea was placed for purification of the outward body;
- Redemption: Acknowledgement of the atonement as one comes to the inner court, and ponders the altar, where sacrifices were daily offered for sins;
- Commitment: Bowing down in the Holy of Holies, at the feet of Jesus the crucified and risen One, whose sacrifice allows us into the very presence of God Himself.

These are the steps by which persons are made ready to hear the gospel in a group setting. The saved, remembering their lost estate, call to mind the great sacrifice of God. The lost, perhaps considering for the first time the gravity of their sin before God, are called upon to look to the cross as their only hope. The commitment called for in the fourth point will coincide with the commitment for which the Evangelist will call when He concludes His message.

The following is a recommended pattern to typify the average revival or evangelistic service:

- The prelude hymns should focus on the cross;
- The first number "should be bright, fast, and enthusiastic, one that will make the choir want to march in smiling and make the people want to stand up and sing" (Bisagno);
- The rhythm of the singing should slow in preparation for the preaching;

159

- Finally, when the invitation is given, the song chosen should plead for souls in the same fashion as the invitation of the Evangelist.

Keith recalled the joy that he had in working with Rick Stone at an evangelism meeting:

> "Rick started with fast loud hand clapping music that even lost people who had never been in church could sing. In a matter of moments he slowed the tempo. By the time the choir sang and he beautifully sang his solo, you could have heard a pin drop. Those youth flooded the aisle when the invitation was given to commit their lives to Christ."[10]

6. The invitation hymn, song, or chorus should flow naturally from the final point in the evangelistic message:

One of the most disheartening aspects in the invitation for anyone who desires to see decisions to be made is when there is a complete disconnect between the sermon and the invitation song. Both Keith and Tom have experienced, unfortunately, the power of God on a sermon, and then a complete disconnect with the invitation song. The musician must submit to the leadership of the Preacher in the choice of an invitation hymn. The Bible says, "Let all things be done decently and in order" (1 Cor 14:40).

Sometimes musicians are not adequately gifted to change a predetermined song on the fly. Sometimes they are not willing to change the song, because of all their preparation and practice. The best harvest musicians choose a song during the last five minutes of the message or even during the invitation. The song fits directly with the theme and emphasis of the message, as well as with the invitation. For example, at Riverside Baptist Church in Bixby, Oklahoma, the song leader chose a hymn and sent a text from his cell phone to the pianist and organist toward the end of the sermon. The notes in the hymn books made it easy for them to "play on the fly"

---

[10]Fordham, "Revival Evangelism Music."

without rehearsal—Tom as the evangelist was on cloud nine when he heard the invitation song as it always fit perfectly with his point!

It is at the point of decision when the Holy Spirit is working the most aggressively—and so is His foe! John Bisagno rightly says that the invitation hymn is the most important hymn of the evening, and should not be thrown in as a boring routine or expected an add-on to every service. If a choir is being used for the invitation, it should be practiced more than any of the other pieces.

Intense prayer and concern ought to be on the heart and in the face of the Music Evangelist, the musicians, the choir, or worship team, as concerns the invitation. The invitation is a solemn time. There ought to be no distractions from God wooing souls to Himself. The songs should be played and sung respectfully and reverently, in a spirit of prayer.

7. The invitation singing should never involve a break in the evangelist's conclusion, but rather flow out of and complement his conclusion:

Everything in the evangelistic service, from the prelude and welcome to the final amen should focus on the invitation. The evangelist's sermon, from the opening sentence to the final plea should focus on the invitation. Therefore, it is extremely important that there be no break in the flow from the sermon into the invitation hymn. The preacher should not withdraw from his position, unless to stand closer to the audience. The musicians should rise quietly when the Evangelist gives them a signal or enters into the invitation. Frank Shivers wrote:

"The invitation must tie in with the sermon without any break or delay. I like for the musician to get in place while I am praying at the end of my message and begin playing the invitational song quietly. I instruct them that I always have a prayer at the close of my message during which time I would like for them to move to the instruments and begin playing softly"[11]

8. Several further recommendations:

- All musicians ought to be invited to pray daily with the revival team for God to move during the services.
- If a special revival theme song is to be learned, consider following the eight guidelines of Charles Alexander:

    1. Easy to learn
    2. There must be a simple, easy, flowing melody.
    3. A small range, not much over an octave.
    4. A picture in every line of every verse.
    5. The words must be simple, but full of faith, hope and promise.
    6. If the first verse does not go well, I go no further with it, and sing something else.
    7. It must be scripturally based.
    8. It must move people to Christ.[12]

- Maintain variety in music to avoid monotony; for example, change of key, change of rhythm, or use of antiphonal singing.
- A revival is not the time to use untested musicians.
- Begin on time; and beware of ending too late unless there is a clear move of God.
- Don't allow special numbers, announcements, or special speakers to rob the Evangelist of the time he needs to preach and give an invitation.
- Be confident in leading music; look straight into the eyes of the people, God will bless the words as they sink into the hearts of those who sing or hear the music.

God always blesses the honest efforts of His people. He knows that you can only do as you are able. We all learn on the fly, as it were. And we all make mistakes. Above all, be faithful to the Word, do your best, and the Lord Jesus Christ will bless your efforts.

---

[11]Frank Shivers, *Revivals 101: A Concise "How To" Manual on Revivals* (Sumter, SC: Victory Hill, 2008), 45.

[12]Helen C. Alexander and J. Kennedy Maclean, *Charles M. Alexander*, 61-68.

CHAPTER TWELVE

REVIVAL PREPARATION

"Revival preparation is a must if a church is to experience the fullness of God's blessings, during a scheduled revival crusade. I'm sure that you share my desire to see God bless in such a way that He will make a tremendous impact, not only in your church family, but in your whole city as well."

Keith Fordham

The need for revival preparation begins with Jesus. Luke is the biographer that recorded that Jesus sent out seventy others in evangelism (Luke 10:1-24), sometime after he sent out the twelve (Luke 9:1-6). In this second sending, Luke included several administrative insights into the narrative:

> "After these things the Lord appointed seventy others also, and sent them two by two before His face into every city and place where He Himself was about to go. Then He said to them, 'The harvest truly *is* great, but the laborers *are* few; therefore pray the Lord of the harvest to send out laborers into His harvest'" (Luke 10:1-2).

In reading these verses, our minds may naturally focus on the seventy others, as well as on the important saying of Jesus, which is a parallel of Matthew 9:37-38. Several other important points come out of these verses. First, Jesus was called "Lord" in verse 1. Then He called God the Father "Lord of the harvest" in verse 2. The absolute supremacy and deity of Christ did not cause Him to shrink from sending out his disciples "two by two before His face."

Christ's absolute supremacy, also stated in Matthew 28:18, did not negate the fact that the disciples were sent to prepare the way for

163

Him. The words "before His face" are reminiscent of the ministry of John the Baptist. He was sent "To prepare the way of the LORD" as prophesied in Isaiah 40:3 (cited in Luke 7:27). Again, the use of the word LORD in Isaiah 40:3 corresponds with the use of "Lord" in Luke 10:1.

Now, John's way of preparing the way for Jesus was to proclaim repentance for the forgiveness of sins (Luke 3:3). John was a revivalist. However, in Luke 10 there is a difference. In preparation for the visit of Jesus the disciples were to declare, "The kingdom of God is at hand." The rulership of God in the lives of individuals was drawing near. Luke drew a parallel between the ministry of John the Baptist and that of the seventy disciples. Both were preparing the way of the Lord.

More interestingly, is the fact that, just as God sovereignly predetermined to work through John the Baptist, so God sovereignly predetermines to use His people to "Go before His face" to bring the Gospel to lost people. When He sends us out, it is not in some haphazard way. Jesus sends us out with vibrant intentionality and clear instructions.

In Luke 10:1 "seventy others" were sent to every city and place where Jesus was about to go. They were, as it were, his advance team. The sovereign Lord desired, determined, and sent out His disciples as His advance team!

Now, hypothetically speaking, does Christ really need an advance team? Of course not! But in His divine will, this course of action was part of His plan. Does Christ really need us to cooperate with Him so that He can save the souls of people to His glory? No. He can and does save them all by Himself. But by His divine will, He planned that salvation should be preached by the mouth of His disciples (Acts 15:7). So, He commissioned His people with a message of preparation and salvation "to all nations" (Luke 24:47). If God Who became flesh needed advance teams for His ministry, today's evangelists also need "advance teams" to prepare for a harvest ministry!

In that regard, Doctor Luke also touched on revival preparation when discussing the ministry of Paul in Acts 28:

> "So when they had appointed him a day, many came to him at *his* lodging, to whom he explained and solemnly testified of the kingdom of God, persuading them concerning Jesus from both the Law of Moses and the Prophets, from morning till evening. And some were persuaded by the things which were spoken, and some disbelieved" (Acts 28:23-24).

Now, we notice several things from these verses:

- While most of Paul's ministry entailed various levels of impromptu evangelism, when he was on house arrest it became even more intentional, and he needed to prepare
- Because Paul was on house arrest, it is certain that others of his team members, not under house arrest, had to help him with preparation
- Resulting from Paul's and his team's preparation:
    1. Many came
    2. At the appointed time
    3. For the appointed length of time—all day long!
    4. To the appointed location—his lodging!
- Further, and perhaps most importantly, because of Paul's and his team's preparation eternal decisions were made for Jesus—"some were persuaded" to come to Christ!

So in these several verses, we find the exact reasons why a revival needs proper preparation. If it is the desire of the pastor to reach as many as possible, then he needs to prepare. Why? So that many will come to hear about Jesus. Further, they need to know the exact date, time, and location where they are to come. This is the result of proper preparation.

In the Bible the Greek verb *tasso* (τάσσω) is used at the beginning of Luke 28:23. *Tasso* means to "arrange, appoint, order." If a proper meeting is to be held, it needs to be arranged and ordered. Imagine, pastor, changing the time for the Sunday morning service without telling your congregation. The turnout would not be very good. Now, imagine inviting lost people and unchurched people to come to a weeknight revival service that they know nothing about. If it is difficult for church members to change service times when they are forewarned, it is even more difficult to get people to come to church who have never been there before. For a revival or any other type of meeting to be successful, there needs to be proper publicity, and for proper publicity, there needs to be proper organization.

Now why organize a revival? Revivals rightly done, for the right motives are a valuable tool which the Lord has used and does use to:

- Bring people to himself;
- Unify and enthuse the church about evangelism and fulfilling the Great Commission;
- Provide many ancillary blessings upon the church, such as growth in membership, growth in community awareness of the church, and growth in giving.

Amazing is the fact that research has shown that churches that have revivals lead more people to Christ than those that do not:

- Churches not conducting revivals:
  - 1/43 ratios baptism per resident members
- Churches conducting revivals:
  - 1/24 ratio baptism per resident members
- Churches conducting revivals with Preparation:
  - 1/19 ratio baptism per resident members[1]

It must first be noted that this study was not small in scope. It took into account information from 3,514 churches, made up of 1,028,669 members, and including 36,432 total baptisms. Nor was it archaic, the study was conducted using statistics from 2001. In the same study done for the year 2011 with 2, 081 churches reporting, the ratios were the same.

[1]Research, Georgia Baptist Convention, 2001.

So, it was shown that churches that conducted revivals with preparation baptize more than twice the number of people than those who do not conduct revivals. Could this mean that churches that have revivals have a greater evangelistic spirit, or that churches that have a greater evangelistic spirit have revivals? Either case is valid. Sleepy churches wake up to the need for evangelism and revival, and lively churches are made more dynamic by hosting a God-called evangelist for revival services. Having an evangelist and revival are like throwing gas on a fire.

The power of the revival resides in the Holy Spirit speaking in, with, and by the Word of Christ to bring souls to repentance (Rom 1:16; 1 Cor 1:18). So technically, revival preparation saves no one. However, proper preparation of a revival allows more people to come under the hearing of the Word, and it is the Word of Christ that saves souls. Therefore, God can and does use revival preparation to draw sinners into the church or venue to hear the Gospel and be saved!

So, once that a pastor feels led to conduct a revival, what steps should he take in organizing for a revival?

1. Assay the Feel of the Church

The first step is to assay the feel of the church. If you are a new pastor to a church or have never conducted a revival in your church during your tenure there, the first step in preparing for revival is to speak with your deacons individually. In doing so, you will assay their view towards revivals, and you will probably hear positives or negatives toward revivals held in the past. You will need to keep these things in mind as you prepare your church for revival. It is quite likely that one of your deacons or perhaps another leader in your church will be very excited by the prospect of organizing a revival. Begin to organize from the very beginning with that person who is excited about it!

2. Determine What Kind of Revival

Second, determine what kind of a revival that God is calling you to arrange. You may want to dream and pray with that excited person. Ask yourself:

- When was the last time that there was a revival in our church or in our town?
- Do we want to get other churches involved?
- Do I have good relationships with like-minded pastors in town so that we can cooperate in a harvest event?
- What is the best venue for a revival: is it our church building, a tent, a barn or shed, the high school auditorium, or an athletic field?

Be creative! Get excited! Have fun! Try new things! While it is important to be realistic, especially if there are extra costs involved in renting a tent or paying for a location, having a bigger vision for reaching the lost may be exactly what God is wanting from you. Begin to pray with and seek the advice of others.

Planning a single church revival avoids many of the issues that are involved in planning a multi-church revival. If you plan a single church revival, people will come from other churches to visit if there is proper publicity. Whatever you hear from others, do not become so discouraged that you do nothing!

3. Set a Date

Third, you need to set a date. Be sure to set a date at least six months in advance. Even in a small church, it will take several months to determine who should be on the Revival Committee and to begin meeting. Be sure to give yourself enough time for all the unknown administrative details that will come up. Here are some questions you may want to keep in mind:

- What will be a good time of the year to get the evangelist that we are hoping to invite?

168

- Is the weather suitable for a tent revival, and is a tent available at that time?—Tents tend to draw attention to the event, as it is something novel and different as people drive by the church property
- Is there another major event in town which will either help or hinder attendance at a revival, such as a county fair, town carnival, kid's camp, graduation event, etc.

Set a date appropriate to your church and your town.

4. Contact an Evangelist

Fourth, once a date has been determined, then it is important to contact a God-called Evangelist. Please consider as highest priority the need to invite an Ephesians 4:11 Evangelist. These are men who are called, equipped, and experienced in harvest evangelism meetings. It only makes sense to call them. Ninety-nine percent of the time an evangelist is used, public professions of faith are made! Wisdom from the Lord is needed to invite the right man. The pastor should know personally, or by the recommendation of reputable people, that the evangelist and his evangelism team are worthy in every sense of the word: sound in doctrine, cooperative in attitude, sane in methods, morally upright, and effective as an evangelistic preacher or musician.

One way of finding evangelists is the Conference of Southern Baptist Evangelists (COSBE) website: www.sbcevangelist.org. Some state conventions also have associations of Southern Baptist evangelists. Your state Director of Evangelism should also be a good resource.

5. Get a Revival Preparation Manual

Fifth, ask the evangelist for a revival preparation manual. If he has one, be sure to prioritize his guidelines and emphases. There is also a "Resource Manual" on the COSBE website that can be of assistance. The North American Mission Board also published a helpful revival preparation guide. Purchase or print enough planbooks or manuals for everyone on the staff, all committee chairmen, and for all those on the Revival Committee. The planbooks normally cover items such as cost and timing of administrative details.

You may also want to consider further items:

- Invite the evangelist to preach at your church from 3-6 months prior to revival to enthuse the church;
- Inviting the evangelist to meet with your Revival Committee 3 months before the revival to discuss the importance of preparation, and to highlight those areas of interest to him
- Invite the musicians to come during a separate service in advance of the meeting, so that they can create additional interest
- Begin to work with the revival preparation team of the evangelist, and be sure to follow the advice that they give or utilize his plan book. Note a number of state conventions offer this service free or at a nominal fee.

Of course, the availability of the evangelist or musicians prior to the meeting will depend on their schedule and transportation costs. But every effort should be made to prepare the congregation for the big event.

Billy Graham has said that 90% of the work of a crusade takes place prior to the crusade event. Then there is the 10% of work which is follow-up, which is also very important. Whatever you do, please make preparation for the revival one of your top priorities, as well as a top priority for your staff and the entire church body.

6. Develop a Revival Countdown Schedule

Six, develop a monthly and weekly countdown of administrative items that need to be accomplished each month and week prior to the revival. The administrative items may seem overwhelming (if you are following a Revival Planning Guide), so you will need to pair it down with your Revival Committee to fit for you situation, and to consider what should be done when it should be done. It is recommended that you organize the major items monthly from

Month Minus 6 to Month Minus 3. Then 8-weeks away from the revival, items should be listed week-by-week and checked off the list. Administrative details will be helpful for a Revival Committee to discuss in their early meetings (Month Minus 6) for feasibility for your church, to itemize as to who should accomplish the task, and then place it on the Revival Calendar.

7. Gather and Organize Publicity

Seven, gather and organize the publicity. Order from the evangelist all the types and sizes of publicity material that he has. These need to be reviewed by the committee so that timing and budgetary decisions can be made. Will you print publicity materials in house or have them printed elsewhere? Will a mass mailing be sent out, and if so, who will author, proof, and print them? When will they be dropped into the mail, and how much will postage cost? Will any banners be made to publicize the revival, if so, how large, one or two-sided, and where and when will they be made? In order to be organized for radio announcements, newspaper articles, billboards, yard signs, t-shirts, bumper stickers, and placing posters in prominent places, initial legwork and cost analysis will need to be done. How many posters will you need? A good rule of thumb is to order twice as many posters as you think, unless you are accustomed to advertising a revival.

8. Work with the Finance Committee

Eight, the finance committee will need to meet to go over the recommendations for costs:

- The rental of a tent or venue
- The base gift to be given to the Evangelist, over and above the love offering and the cost of travel, food, and lodging
- The gift for the musicians (as applicable)
- The cost of publicity (banners, posters, mailings, newspaper advertisements, radio spots, etc.).

Remember the role of the finance committee, and do not get discouraged when bringing up the costs associated with the revival. It is often helpful for the revival committee to know what they have to work with, so that they can pair down their ideas into reasonable costs for the finance committee, as well as be creative in cutting costs without cutting publicity.

9. Plan Your Work, and Work Your Plan

Ninth, the motto for the last two months must be "Plan your work, and work your plan." If all plans are in place prior to the last two months before the revival, then it will make it much easier for those who are helping out in various roles. All the publicity items should be placed on the timeline, as to when they are printed, when they are compiled, and when they are sent or put up. There will always be things that fall between the cracks. So, if the known items are organized, then the administrative headaches can be saved for the unknown items.

Generally speaking, the more creative the publicity, the more impact it will have in order to bring in more people to hear the Gospel proclaimed by a God-called Evangelist. It is all definitely worth it.

During the countdown of the last two months, remember also to keep the revival before the people of the church:

- Place prayer requests in the bulletin weekly
- Send letters from the pastor and evangelist to church members and prospects
- Place posters within the church building with the dates of the revival
- Create "Prayer Tents" one month prior to the meeting so that families can begin to pray for the meetings at meal times
- Prepare a special 30-day prayer countdown for the working of the Lord during the revival
- Coordinate special youth and children's events as preparation for the revival

- Organize cottage prayer meetings one month before the revival
- Send out letters to your Sunday School teachers, for the special lesson that teaches about revival (see Keith Fordham's planbook)
- Include PowerPoint presentations or videos about the upcoming revival in your services.

Most of all, be excited for a great time from the Lord! The church people will be working together to further the Great Commission and there is much excitement as people see the banners go up, the tent go up, the posters go up. People get excited when they see that their church is doing something, and it becomes contagious.

Then, by the grace of God, on the appointed days, many will come to the church, hear the Gospel, and some will be saved!

CONCLUSION

The church of today is largely under house arrest. We have turned our backs on the holy office of the Evangelist. We have closed our ears to his plea for souls. We have despised his invitation to respond to the Great Commission. And in so doing, we have closed our ears to God Himself.

In our sophistication and in our great learning, we have turned aside. We prefer reading statistics on the latest trends in churches than wielding God's mighty sword. Our professors have turned aside. Our textbooks have turned aside. And the Evangelist and His work have been buried under mountains of rationalization. We have turned aside to the vain philosophies of this world, and have shown little regard for the office of the Evangelist. And in so doing, we have placed our churches and the gospel of Jesus on house arrest. We have deafened our ears to the cry of lost souls on the highways and byways.

Could not God in His sovereignty pour forth His power from heaven and call out a mighty army of Evangelists? Christ is still calling in His still small voice to thousands of young men across this nation and across the world, calling them to be sold-out for the cause of the gospel. Are we listening to His voice? Are we readying ourselves, our churches, and our sons to listen to God's voice calling out? Let's once again find worth in the office of Evangelist, and sacrifice to send our sons and daughters out into the fight for lost souls.

The only hope for our nation or for any people is found in the gospel proclaimed. The only hope for releasing the church from house arrest is once again to bestow honor upon the New Testament office of Evangelist. He is the God-called vessel to move us out of the pews and into the highways and byways. The Evangelist was chosen by Christ to sit in the leadership of His New Testament church, to stir the coals and keep the fires of the Great Commission burning in every local church. Let every local church place an Evangelist on their leadership team!

To honor the office of the Evangelist, it will take intentionality. It will mean a move away from the status quo. All the forces of the Enemy will stand against us, if we decide to unleash the office of the Evangelist within our churches. It is worth the fight, as thousands and millions of lost souls are at stake. It is worth the fight, when the spirituality of our sons and daughters is at stake. We have no choice but to fight, and fight we must.

We must use Evangelists. We must make ready our churches to honor his message. We must ready our towns to greet him upon his arrival. We must get serious about the Great Commission, and let this Great Commission leader lead!

We must break out of our lethargy. We cannot and must not do business as usual. We must return the reigns of the local church to the Lord of the Church. We must do it His way. We must take our lead from Him. Let us not be stirred by the "best practices" of the church down the street, but rather from the work of the Holy Spirit throughout the pages of the Book of Acts. We must allow Jesus Christs to lead His church in His way!

Submit therefore to the Master's voice, right now! Repent, right now! Ask God to give you both the wisdom and the courage necessary to honor the office of the Evangelist! Now is the time! Today is the day! Ask Him right now!

Appendix One

"Shamgar's Oxgoad"[1]

T. Dewitt Talmadge (1832-1902)

"Shamgar, with his unaided arm, howsoever muscular, and with that humble instrument made for agricultural purposes, and never constructed for combat, could not have wrought such victory. It was Omnipotence above and beneath and back of and at the point of the ox-goad. Before that battle was over, the plowman realized this, and all the six hundred Philistines realized it, and all who visited the battlefield afterward appreciated it. I want in heaven to hear the story, for it can never be fully told on earth—perhaps some day may be set apart for the rehearsal, while all heaven listens—the story of how God blessed awkward and humble instrumentalities.

"Many an evangelist has come into a town given up to worldliness. The pastors say to the evangelist, 'We are glad you have come, but it is a hard field, and we feel sorry for you. The members of our churches play progressive euchre (cards) and go to the theatre and bet at the horse races, and gaiety and fashion have taken possession of the town. We have advertised your meetings, but are not very hopeful. God bless you.'

"This evangelist takes his place on platform or pulpit. He never graduated at college, and there are before him twenty graduates of the best universities. He never took one lesson in elocution, and there are before him twenty trained orators. Many of the ladies present are graduates of the highest female seminaries, and one slip in grammar or one mispronunciation will arouse a suppressed giggle. Amid the general chill that pervades the house, the unpretending evangelist opens his Bible and takes for his text, 'Lord, that my eyes may be opened.'

[1]T. Dewitt Talmadge, *500 Selected Sermons*, vol. 3, (Grand Rapids: Baker, 1978), 155.

"Opera-glasses in the gallery curiously scrutinize the speaker. He tells in a plain way the story of the blind man, tells two or three touching anecdotes, and the general chill gives way before a strange warmth. A classical hearer who took the first honor at Yale, and who is a prince of proprieties, finds his spectacles become dim with a moisture suggestive of tears. A worldly mother who has been bringing up her sons and daughters in utter godlessness, puts her handkerchief to her eyes and begins to weep. Highly educated men who came to criticize and pick to pieces and find fault, bow on their gold-headed canes. What is that sound from under the gallery? It is a sob, and sobs are catching; and all along the wall, and all up and down and audience, there is deep emotion, so that when at the close of the service anxious souls are invited to special seats, or the inquiry-room; they come up by scores and kneel and repent and rise up pardoned; the whole town is shaken, and places of evil amusement are sparsely attended, and rum-holes lose their patrons, and the churches are thronged, and the whole community is cleansed and elevated and rejoiced.

"What power did the evangelist bring to bear to capture that town for righteousness? Not one brilliant epigram did he utter; not one graceful gesture did he make; not one rhetorical climax did he pile up. But there was something about him that people had not taken in the estimate when they prophesied the failure of that work. They had not taken into the calculation the omnipotence of the Holy Ghost. It was not the flash of a Damascus blade. It was God, before and behind and all around the ox-goad.

APPENDIX TWO

Practical Uses of Evangelists for the Pastor,
Church, University, Seminary, and Denominational Entity

Keith Fordham

- Learn who your Evangelists are. Go to www.sbcEvangelist.org.
- Use Evangelists on Pastor's Conferences, State Evangelism Conferences, and Associational Evangelism Meetings. This is one of the few venues where pastors can hear how Christ has gifted the Evangelists, and allow them firsthand knowledge of a tool for their church.
  Note: while each church needs one pastor, every church needs multiple Evangelists. This is why Evangelists need to be heard in settings where many pastors gather.
- Utilize the Evangelist's vast experiences on denominational, state, and local committees to assist in Biblical strategies to reach the lost.
- Use an Evangelist to extend the invitation for VBS, Wild Game Suppers, Cantatas, Dramas, Upward Sports Award Services, etc… It is amazing at the difference it makes.
- Use the Evangelists' materials. Apply them to your local situation. They have specialties like prayer, witness and counselor training to follow-up, and just plain practical advice which can be most helpful.
- Use the "Revival Method" to plant churches. It is the most effective method used over the past 60 years. Here is a synopsis of the Revival Method of church planting:
  o For 10 weeks have outside church groups do census, door to door visitation, door hangers, backyard Bible clubs, block parties, ICE teams, special events etc…

- o   In addition, do phone surveys and media free and purchased that is available.
- o   On the final week do a VBS at the new church sight in the morning and a revival at night. Often a tent or community building is used.
- o   I know of 86 people who joined the first week in one location and 205 in another.

- Use mass evangelism on the local church level as well as the city to nationwide level. Nationwide unified mass evangelism will work in the local church, local Association, State Convention and nationwide. We need to work together.

- Revival should be promoted by the North American Mission Board just as Vacation Bible School is promoted by LifeWay! The synergy of simultaneous revival will boost all evangelism throughout any denomination or nation.

- Nearly everything I have learned about, evangelism, revival preparation, and outreach came to me through NAMB. My pastors used it and taught it to me. NAMB had 36 pieces of material for the pastor and Evangelist. Now it only has a handful. Please take up the baton for Mass Evangelism.

- Most pastors learn the practical side of what works in evangelism in their local church through the Evangelists they have in their pulpits.

- Insights that cover an entire denomination come from Evangelists who constantly travel and work with different churches. Evangelists see the need for Great Commission Education that gives men the practical tools to work with in college and Seminary.

- Evangelists should be on all trustee boards and committees of entities that in anyway promote evangelism, so that they can give their input.

- Seminaries need to utilize evangelists in Chapel and in classes whenever possible.

- Evangelistic, revival, preaching should be taught by men with at least 30 years in evangelism.

- Evangelists are experts in giving all kinds of invitations to receive Christ and counseling. This resource needs to be tapped.

APPENDIX THREE

"Taking a Revival Offering"[2]

John R. Bisagno

From:

"Attitude! Remember that word. In the final analysis, the success of the offering depends upon the attitude of the one who takes it.

"After spending over twelve years in the evangelistic field and watching hundreds of men take offerings, it seems that the most important factor is this: Does the pastor really want a visiting evangelist to get a good offering? If he does, he can get it. I know many pastors and full-time evangelists who consistently conduct revivals. I believe that I speak authoritatively when I say I do not know a man who would not be satisfied with the offering that the people gave, whether large or small, if the pastor did all he could to take it. If he genuinely wants to get a good offering and seeks it in a positive way, with some preparations outlined herein, a good offering will be assured. But if he fails in some of the simple mechanics of taking a good offering and does not really want the man to have a good offering, the people will recognize it and will not respond.

"In inviting a visiting preacher to conduct a revival, the pastor should consider several things. If the church is small and unable to give sizable offerings, an outside singer should not be employed. A 60-40 percent division of the offering will not mean a worthy amount for either of God's servants in the event the offering is small. In this case it is best to use a local man to do the music, with the understanding that he will be given an honorarium from the budget.

"By all means, it should be clearly understood in advance who is going to get what. It is both dishonest and impractical to receive a love offering in

[2] John Bisagno, *The Power of Positive Evangelism*, 38-42, 42-45, 45-47. Used by permission. Bold text has been updated.

the name of the evangelist and give part to the building fund or church treasury, if this was not clearly stated night by night as the offering was received.

"Is an honorarium to be given to the organist and pianist? If so, it should be arranged for in a business meeting or in the planning of the annual church budget, but clearly defined and agreed upon *ahead of time*. It should not be taken from the love offering for the visiting preacher.

"One of the most common mistakes made in receiving love offerings, or any type of offering for that matter, is to presume that we must protect the people's pocketbook by not trying very hard. If you make up your mind to get a good offering, one that will be a true expression of love and a blessing to the recipient, then ask for it positively, prayerfully, and with great anticipation. The people will protect their own pocketbooks.

"If you do it negatively, the people, the evangelist, and the Lord will be embarrassed. I have seen men take offerings when it was obvious that they really weren't trying and didn't care how much the love offering was. They always hand it to the evangelist and say, "My, we are sorry it couldn't have been more." They really weren't sorry at all. They didn't want it to be more or they would have tried.

"Perhaps they were afraid of their people or were afraid they would give too much and hurt the church budget, but remember, you cannot out give God. You do your people a great service when you lead them to give liberally and let them know you expect them to do so. The Lord will bless your church as you bless the men of God who preach from your pulpit. Our people will not give more than they can. Let them worry about that; you need not protect them.

"Love offerings that are a guaranteed amount in the budget are no love offerings at all. I, personally, would rather receive **$1,500** that was a genuine expression of the love of the people who gave all they could, than **$3,000** that was a 'fee' paid to hire a preacher for the week.

"When you discuss the forthcoming revival with your evangelist, discuss the manner of the receiving and dividing of the love offering frankly. Don't embarrass him by expecting him to bring up the subject. Tell him your church's usual policy and ask him his desires. When you accepted the call to the pastorate of the church, you probably discussed the salary with the pulpit committee. You should do the same with the men you invite. This is good sense and good business. Don't pretend that it isn't important and that just anything will do. It is important and just anything *won't* do. The care of our family, education of our children, and payment of our bills are important to all of us. Have a clear understanding and do the best you can in the offering. I have never had to apologize for an offering I gave a man, or for any cause. It is with a great deal of pride that I hand a good-sized offering check to every man that preaches from my pulpit. God blesses a cheerful giver. He likewise blesses a church that expects to do big in the matter of the love offering.

"If you lead your people to think negatively and to give small, the chickens will come home to roost in your whole ministry and church. God must make big men for the big places. Part of our Christian 'bigness' is our genuine desire to share. Make up your mind whether you <u>really</u> want this man to have a good offering. If you do, let your people know it, and they will never give an offering that you will be embarrassed to hand to a visiting preacher.

"How much offering is enough for a visiting evangelist? In answering this, many factors should be considered. For denominational workers, pastors, and missionaries who have a steady income from other sources, it is obvious that less is required than for a full-time evangelist with no other means of livelihood. Whether the pastor of a large church with a large income or not, I do not know of any of God's men who are overpaid. Men with big incomes and big churches usually have big expenses. Most **$60,000 to $100,000** a year men could be making **$200,000** a year if their talents were dedicated to the business world. You do not need to protect the people from giving too much, nor do you need to protect the visiting preacher from receiving too much.

"...It is important that a visiting preacher begin a revival on Sunday morning in order to reach the morning crowd and get them back...."

[Keith Fordham: "Most churches want Sunday through Wednesday meetings. This leaves Thursday and Saturday off for travel. Friday is office work and catch up day. This kind of arrangement means the evangelist can hold 30 revivals a year during key revival weeks. He can give from one week to four weeks of his time for mission work and also have time for Bible studies, evangelism conferences, and the Southern Baptist Convention. Indeed, he will have a full year, but not all weeks are paying weeks. Many items that the pastor gets free as office stationary, secretarial help, stamps, outside income above the salary from weddings and funerals must be considered. An evangelist's budget is often like that of a small church and yet it has a worldwide ministry with a budget like that of a large church."]

"...A visiting evangelist, to the contrary, often must pay his own travel expenses, convention expenses, buy his own envelopes, and pay for his own retirement, health insurance, utilities, secretarial help, pictures, stationary, and so on.

"In the event of a prolonged sickness, he has no income.... the evangelist would have to receive around **$2,000-$3,500** before any real love offering, over and above basic expenses was given. All of these and other factors should be considered in receiving a love offering. This must be explained; publicly, to the people. Too often the people are never told that the evangelist is a full-time worker without a guaranteed income.

"You should at all times be positive in the receiving of the offering. Tell the people that we have a wonderful man and it is an honor for our church to have him lead us. This is certainly not high pressure and no one will rebel at this positive approach. To the contrary, the businessmen in your church will think less of him and less of you if you pass him off as a nobody to whom they may give just anything. Never use a negative approach in the receiving of the offering. If you tell your people that this man has twenty-nine kids, a broken-down automobile, and a sick wife, they will not respond. People like to be identified with success, not misery. They will give much more if the evangelist is presented as a highly successful man whom God has blessed mightily. Neither evangelist nor pastor should ever put on the 'poor act,' nor should they 'strut their stuff.' The positive approach should always be used.

"Certainly never make the mistake of telling the evangelist you will send the offering later. You like to get paid on payday—so does he. When the revival closes payday for the visiting evangelist has arrived. Instruct the church treasurer to have the money counted, make the check, and present it immediately at the end of the services. He probably needs it then, not next week.

"With your evangelist, your treasurer, your finance committee, and your people, the difference between the expense offering and love offering should be very thoroughly defined. The expenses for the special nights, publicity, travel to and from the city for the evangelist, motel, and meals should be taken from the expenses. It is best to have an amount set aside in the budget of the church to care for these expenses....

"...Everything that is given loose and through love offering envelopes should go for the love offering....

"...In the event that the evangelist is eating part or all of his meals out, he should be instructed to sign the ticket, including tip, and told that the church will take care of this. As your guest, he should be treated as such. Travel expenses to and from the meeting, unless he is going to another campaign, should be taken care of by the church. It is best to write ahead of time and see if he would prefer to have travel money sent in advance. He may need it to come to your church.

"The evangelist should care for his own laundry, cleaning, and long distance telephone calls. **Love offering envelopes, should be provided by the church. The envelopes should be large enough to place a check or $100 bill in without being folded. It is best all checks be made payable to the church, it should be explained that the love offering will all be given to the evangelist in one check from the church.**

"Some pastors, who feel led of God to help an evangelist communicate his needs to others, may provide a list of people from their churches who are interested in that particular evangelist. This should be left up to the pastor, with no pressure from the evangelist."

[Bisagno's chapter continues]

"...Occasionally, the evangelist may augment his ministry and supplement his income through the sale of books. Whether this is acceptable to the local pastor and church should be clearly understood in advance so that he will not be embarrassed by being refused after he arrives. If they are to be sold, it should be done outside of the auditorium and all money handled by the local church. The announcement concerning the sale of books should be made by the local people. This is, of course, a matter to be decided in each situation. In most churches it is entirely acceptable; in some it is not.

"The actual distribution of the envelopes and the use of the offering plates to receive the offering is of tremendous importance. The most common mistake, and one of the worst, is to place offering envelopes in the plates and then pass the plates, announcing that envelopes may be obtained thereby. It is impossible for an individual to stop the offering plate, take out an envelope, fill it out, put money in it, and pass it on. *This should never be done.* People should not be asked to take the envelopes home and fill them out for the next night. There are three reasons why: (1) many of them will not be back the next night; (2) many will give every night, if the offering is taken properly, and will give much more in that way; (3) the majority of the people will leave the envelope at home. Take the offering every night as though that were the only night you were going to take it. Don't mention taking it tomorrow night.

"The second best way to distribute the envelopes is to put them in the pews in the envelope holders and publicly ask everyone to take one before you make the appeal for the offering. The very best way, however, is to place the envelope in the hands of the people ahead of time. This can be done at the door or by asking the ushers to come forward during the early part of the announcement time and give them out. Never ask people to raise their hands for them. You might just as well ask them to take a rattlesnake as to take an envelope. Most will not ask for one, and yet, 90 percent will give if you place an envelope in their hands. I, personally, do not like giving them at the door unless they are stapled to a bulletin or something else they are going to receive anyway. In my opinion the following method, over the years, has been the most successful and the most effortless.

"At the beginning of the announcement period, ask the ushers to go to the end of each row and give ten or fifteen envelopes to the person seated on the aisle. This person will, in turn, pass them down his row, giving each person the opportunity to take one, whether they intend to use it or not. Tell the ushers not to say, 'Do you want one?' It may be that the man on the end will refuse to jump up and down and beg for one, but that the other fifteen people on the row will want one. Extend them to the man and ask him to take one and pass them on. The extras can then be left on the seat at the other end of the row.

"Do not make the appeal for the offering at this time, since you will have more announcements and special music, and much of the good of the appeal will be lost before the offering is taken. Thoroughly distribute the envelopes in this manner, asking the people to wait to fill them out until later in the service.

"When the announcements are made and the last hymn has been sung, the people will stand as the ushers come forward. Remain standing as you make a good appeal, telling them of the needs, the opportunities, and the blessings of giving. Let them see you make your offering. As you fill out your envelope, they will fill out theirs. Then pray and pass the plates.

"'The servant is worthy of his hire.' I have been on the giving and the receiving end of some very good offerings. I admonish you to remember the words of our Lord, who said, 'It is more blessed to give than to receive.' You cannot out give God!"

APPENDIX FOUR

CHARTER

KEITH FORDHAM EVANGELISTIC ASSOCIATION, INC.
UNITED STATES OF AMERICA
STATE OF LOUISIANA
PARRISH JEFFERSON

BE IT KNOWN that on this <u>22</u> day of July in the year of Our Lord Nineteen Hundred and Seventy Four, before me, STUART A. McCLENDON, Notary Public, duly commissioned and qualified in and for the Parish of Jefferson, State of Louisiana, and in the presence of the witnesses hereinafter named and undersigned, personally came and appeared:

KEITH FORDHAM

who declared that availing himself of the provisions of the laws of the State of Louisiana, and, particularly, Louisiana Revised Statute, Title 12, Section 201 in following, he does by these presents form and constitute a non-profit corporation or body politic in law for the objects and purposes and under the agreements and stipulations following, to-wit:

ARTICLE I

The name of the corporation is KEITH FORDHAM EVANGELISTIC ASSOCIATION, INC. and shall have perpetual duration.

ARTICLE II

The corporation is organized for and may engage in missionary, charitable, literary and educational activities, however, its primary purpose shall be the spreading of the Gospel of Jesus Christ through the preaching of His Word, winning lost men to a saving knowledge of Him, and using every available means in promulgating a witness of His saving grace. This may be done through and including the conducting of revival services, Bible conferences, printed literature, and the support of missionaries and the use of mass media. The corporation may engage in any religious, charitable, literary or educational activity in the furtherance of these ends, but is specifically prohibited from carrying on otherwise than as an insubstantial part of its activities, activities which are not in furtherance of one or more purposes, exempt by law.

ARTICLE III

The registered office of the corporation shall be 213 Imperial Office Bldg., 3301 N. Causeway Blvd., Metairie, Louisiana 70002.

ARTICLE IV

The registered agents of the corporation shall be:

> STUART A. McCLENDON
> 213 Imperial Office Bldg.
> 3301 N. Causeway Blvd.
> Metairie, Louisiana 70002
>
> RICHARD L. GREENLAND
> 213 Imperial Office Bldg.
> 3301 N. Causeway Blvd.
> Metairie, Louisiana 70002

ARTICLE V

The name and address of the incorporator is as follows:

> KEITH FORDHAM
> 3912 Mirabeau Avenue
> New Orleans, Louisiana

ARTICLE VI

The corporation is organized on a non-stock basis and all persons to be considered for membership must meet the qualifications set forth in the By-Laws and must profess faith in Jesus Christ as Savior and subscribe to the doctrinal statement.

ARTICLE VII

All of the corporate powers of the corporation shall be vested in a Board of Directors composed of not less than three nor more than nine persons, all of whom must be members in good standing. The Board of Directors shall elect its own officers who shall also be the officers of the corporation and who shall serve at the pleasure of the Board of Directors and may be members of the Board of Directors themselves. The first members of the Board of Directors shall be:

KEITH FORDHAM	JAMES RAY WALDROP
SHIRLEY FORDHAM	MRS. A. D. FORDHAM
A. D. FORDHAM	

ARTICLE VIII

The Board of Directors shall elect and fix the compensation of a President, Vice-President and Secretary-Treasurer of the corporation who shall also hold the same offices on the Board of Directors.

ARTICLE IX

The first Board of Directors shall serve for one year from the date of incorporation or until their successors are duly qualified and appointed and directors shall serve until death, resignation, or removal by majority vote of the Board. The first Board of Directors is composed of the following individuals, who shall hold the following offices:

KEITH FORDHAM, President
3912 Mirabeau Avenue
New Orleans, Louisiana

JAMES RAY WALDROP, Vice-President
Lot 2-A, Bulldog Drive
Route 5
Griffin, Georgia 30223

SHIRLEY FORDHAM, Secretary-Treasurer
3912 Mirabeau Avenue
New Orleans, Louisiana

A.D. Fordham
343 Pineridge Drive
Forest Park, Georgia 30050

Mrs. A.D. Fordham
343 Pineridge Drive
Forest Park, Georgia 30050

ARTICLE X

No part of net earnings of this corporation shall ever inure to the benefit of any donor, member, director or officer of the corporation or any private individual, and no donor, member, director or officer of the corporation or any private individual shall be entitled to share in the distribution of any of the corporate assets. Upon the dissolution, any assets of the corporation must be distributed to one or more organizations recognized by the Internal Revenue Service as one organized exclusively for religious, charitable, scientific, literary or educational purposes.

THUS DONE AND PASSED, in duplicate originals, in my notaries office in the City of Metairie, State of Louisiana, on the day, month and year first hereinabove written in the presence of BERTIE BLEDSOE and ALICE JOHNSTON, competent witnesses who have hereunto subscribed their names together with me, Notary, and the said appeared after due reading of the whole.

WITNESSES:

_____   _____
BERTIE BLEDSOE   KEITH FORDHAM

_____
ALICE JOHNSTON

_____
NOTARY PUBLIC

BY-LAWS
OF
KEITH FORDHAM EVANGELISTIC ASSOCIATION, INC.

The following by-laws, adopted by the Board of Directors at a meeting at Metairie, Louisiana, on the 29-day of July, 1974 shall govern the business of the organization except as the same may be, from time to time, abridged or amended.

Article I - Name and Status

Sec. 1. The name of this non-profit corporation as stated in its articles of incorporation is 'Keith Fordham Evangelistic Association, Inc.'

Article II - Purpose

Sec. 1. *Scope.* Keith Fordham Evangelistic Association, Inc. is organized exclusively for religious, educational, and charitable purposes.

Sec. 2. *Method of attaining religious and educational purposes.* The religious and educational purposes of Keith Fordham Evangelistic Association, Inc. shall be accomplished by the adoption and implementation of crusades, revivals and Bible studies that promote and expand the understanding of individuals of religious principles that are set forth in the Bible. Such programs and activities consist of and/or include the conduct of various religious and religious-educational activities such as broadcasting, production and/or distribution of radio or television programs of religious nature, conduct of regularly scheduled public and/or private lectures, sermons and teaching institutes of a religious nature, and the publication and distribution of religious newspapers and magazines, articles, books, brochures and other types of writings.

The foregoing programs and activities shall be based upon and at all times shall be consistent with the following beliefs:

a. The Bible is the mind of Christ, and is the inspired, the only infallible and authoritative word of God.

b. There is one God manifested in three personalities and externally expressed as the Father (the Planner), the Son (the Executor), and the Holy Spirit (the Revealer).

c. The personality of Satan and his present control over unregenerate man does exit.

d. Christianity is based upon belief in:
    1. The deity of our Lord Jesus Christ.
    2. His sinless life.
    3. His miracles.
    4. His vicarious and atoning death through His shed blood.
    5. His bodily resurrection.

6. His ascension to the right hand of the Father.
7. His personal return in power and glory.
8. The fall of man and his lost estate, which makes necessary a rebirth through belief in the Lord Jesus Christ.
9. The reconciliation of man to God by the substitutionary death and shed blood of our Lord Jesus Christ.
10. The resurrection of believers unto ever-lasting life and blessing in Heaven, and the resurrection of unbelievers unto ever-lasting punishment in the torments of Hell.
11. The present ministry of the Holy Spirit, by whose indwelling the Christian is enabled to live a godly life.
12. The Church as the indivisible Body of Christ, bound together by the Holy Spirit, consisting of those who are born again in Christ and for whom He shall come again.
13. Christ's great commission to the Church to go into all the world and preach the Gospel to every creature, baptizing and teaching those who believe.

Sec. 3. *Method of attaining religious, charitable and educational purposes.*

The attainment of Keith Fordham Evangelistic Association, Inc.'s religious, charitable and educational purposes shall be accomplished through means to be determined by the Board of Directors. At the time such purposes are determined, they shall be recorded in the minutes of the Directors' meetings.

Article III - Contributions

Sec. l. Keith Fordham Evangelistic Association, Inc. at the direction of the Board of Directors or the Officers, may receive contributions of money and property from individuals, organizations or corporations.

Article IV - Board of Directors

Sec. l. The Board of Directors shall consist of at least three and no more than nine members.

a. *Initial Board of Directors.* The initial Board of Directors of Keith Fordham Evangelistic Association, Inc. shall consist of five members named in the Articles of Incorporation. The

192

initial members of the Board of Directors shall serve until their resignation, death and removal.

b. *Vacancies on Board of Directors.* Vacancies on the Board of Directors created by the resignation, death or removal of a member of the Board of Directors shall be filled by election of the remaining Directors.

c. *Resignation of Directors.* Any Director may submit his or her resignation as a Director at a meeting of the Board of Directors. Upon acceptance of such resignation by the Board of Directors, such person shall no longer be a Director. Failure to sign the Statement of Faith attached to these by-laws as Exhibit A by any director at or before the annual meeting of the Board of Directors constitutes such Director's resignation from the Board of Directors.

d. *Removal of Directors.* Any Director may be removed by the affirmative vote of two-thirds (2/3) of the Board of Directors.

e. *Election of Additional Directors.* The existing Board of Directors may at any time elect additional Directors to serve under provisions listed above.

f. *Directors Subscription to Statement of Faith.* Each member of the Board of Directors at or before the annual meeting of the Board of Directors shall subscribe to the statement of Faith that is affixed hereto as Exhibit A.

Article V – Officers

Sec. 1. *Number.* The officers of Keith Fordham Evangelistic Association, Inc. shall be a President, one or more Vice-Presidents (the number thereof to be determined by the Board of Directors), a Secretary-Treasurer, each of whom shall be elected by the Board of Directors. Such other officers and assistant officers as may be deemed necessary may be elected or appointed by the Board of Directors. The President of Keith Fordham Evangelistic Association, Inc. may hold only one office. Any two of the other offices may be held by the same person.

Sec. 2. *Election and Term of Office.* The officers of Keith Fordham Evangelistic Association, Inc. to be elected by the Board of Directors shall be elected annually by a majority of the entire Board of Directors. Each officer shall hold office until his successor shall have been duly elected and shall have qualified or until his death or until he shall resign or shall have been removed in the manner hereinafter provided.

Sec. 3. *Removal.* Any officer or agent elected or appointed by the Board of Directors may be removed by a majority of the Board of Directors whenever in its judgment the best interests of Keith Fordham Evangelistic Association, Inc. would be served thereby.

Sec. 4. *Vacancies.* A vacancy in any office because of death, resignation, removal, disqualification or otherwise, may be filled by a majority of the entire Board of Directors for the unexpired portion of the term.

Sec. 5. *President.* The President shall be the principal executive officer of Keith Fordham Evangelistic Association, Inc. and, subject to the control of the Board of Directors, shall in general supervise and control all of the business and affairs of Keith Fordham Evangelistic Association, Inc. He shall, when present preside at all meetings of the Board of Directors. He may sign, with the Secretary or any other proper officer of Keith Fordham Evangelistic Association, Inc. thereunto authorized by the Board of Directors, any deed, mortgages, bonds, contracts, or other instruments which the Board of Directors has authorized to be executed, except in cases where the signing and execution thereof shall be expressly delegated by the Board of Directors or by these by-laws to some other officer or agent of Keith Fordham Evangelistic Association, Inc., or shall be required by law to be otherwise signed or executed; and in general shall perform all duties incident to the office of President and such other duties as may be prescribed by the Board of Directors from time to time.

Sec. 6. *The Vice-President.* In the absence of the President or in the event of his death, inability or refusal to act, the Vice-President (or in the event there be more than one Vice-President; the Vice-President in the order designated at the time of their election, or in the absence of any designation, then in the order of their election) shall perform the duties of the President, and when so acting, shall have all the powers of and be subject to all the restrictions upon the President. Any Vice-

President shall perform such duties as from time to time may be assigned to him by the President, or by the Board of Directors.

Sec. 7. *The Secretary.* The Secretary shall: (a) Keep the minutes of the Board of Directors' meetings in one or more books provided for that purpose; (b) see that all notices are duly given in accordance with the provisions of these by-laws or as required by law; (c) be custodian of the corporate records and of the seal of Keith Fordham Evangelistic Association, Inc. and see that the seal of Keith Fordham Evangelistic Association, Inc. is affixed to all documents the execution of which on behalf of Keith Fordham Evangelistic Association, Inc. under its seal is duly authorized; and (d) in general perform all duties incident to the office of secretary and such other duties as from time to time may be assigned to him by the President or the Board of Directors.

Sec. 8. *The Treasurer.* If required by the Board of Directors, the Treasurer shall give a bond for the faithful discharge of his duties in such sum and with such surety or sureties as the Board of Directors shall determine. He shall: have charge and custody of and be responsible for all funds and securities of Keith Fordham Evangelistic Association, Inc.; receive and give receipts for moneys due and payable to Keith Fordham Evangelistic Association, Inc. from any source whatsoever, and deposit all such moneys in the name of Keith Fordham Evangelistic Association, Inc. in such banks, trust companies or other depositories as shall be selected; and (b) in general perform all of the duties incident to the office of Treasurer and such other duties as from time to time may be assigned to him by the President or by the Board of Directors.

Sec. 9. *Salaries.* The salaries of the officers shall be fixed from time to time by two-thirds (2/3) of the entire Board of Directors present or by vote of proxy and no officer shall be prevented from receiving such salary by reason of the fact that he is also a Director of Keith Fordham Evangelistic Association, Inc.

Sec. 10. *Officers Subscription to Statement of Faith.* Each officer shall each year, upon his or her election by the Board of Directors, subscribe to the Statement of Faith that is affixed hereto as Exhibit A unless said Officer has already signed the Statement as a Director. Failure to sign the Statement constitutes the resignation of such Officer from the office he is holding.

Article VI - Fiscal Year

Sec. 1. *Period.* The fiscal year of the organization shall commence on January 1 and continue until the following December 31.

Sec. 2. *Change.* The incoming officers shall recommend to the Board of Directors any change in the fiscal year deemed necessary; said change shall require a majority vote of the entire Board of Directors.

Article VII - Finances of Keith Fordham Evangelistic Association, Inc.

Sec. 1. *Sources of Funds.* Keith Fordham Evangelistic Association, Inc. shall be supported with contributions of money and property received from foundations, corporations, organizations, groups, or individuals.

Sec. 2. *Deposit of Funds in Bank.* Keith Fordham Evangelistic Association, Inc. funds shall be deposited in a bank account. The Board of Directors shall by appropriate resolution select a depository for Keith Fordham Evangelistic Association, Inc.'s funds and authorize the establishment of a bank account in Keith Fordham Evangelistic Association, Inc.'s name.

Sec. 3. *Audit.* There shall be an audit of the Treasurer's records at the close of each fiscal year. The C.P.A. audit shall be conducted by an auditing firm appointed by the Board of Directors. The Audit shall be completed within ninety (90) days after the close of Keith Fordham Evangelistic Association, Inc.'s fiscal year.

Article VIII - Operating Policies

Sec. 1. *Board of Directors and Operating Policies.* The Board of Directors shall hold monthly meetings to be called by the President by giving at least three (3) days notice, such meetings to fall during the second week of the given month. The Board of Directors shall act on such business matters as are required by the Articles of Incorporation and By-laws, such as approval of the budget, authorization of expenditures of funds, appointment of personnel, appointment of committees, and approval of reports. The Board of Directors shall consider these problems which may be presented to it by the Board members, by a committee, by staff, or by contributors to determine which problems come properly within the purposes of Keith Fordham

Evangelistic Association, Inc. and the way in which Keith Fordham Evangelistic Association, Inc. may deal with such problems. The Board of Directors shall determine what authority shall be delegated to committees.

Sec. 2. *Annual Meeting of Directors.* The annual meeting of the Board of Directors of Keith Fordham Evangelistic Association, Inc. shall be the regular meeting held during the month of April. At such meeting, the Officers of Keith Fordham Evangelistic Association, Inc. shall be elected by the Board of Directors as provided in these By-Laws. The audit of the Treasurer's records shall be presented to the Board of Directors for review and appropriate action, if necessary. Any Director who has not subscribed to the Statement of Faith for the ensuing year shall do so at the annual meeting.

Sec. 3. *Committees.* Keith Fordham Evangelistic Association, Inc.'s program shall be operated by the President, supplemented by activities of the various committees established by the Board of Directors.

Sec. 4. *Ex-officio Status of President.* The President of Keith Fordham Evangelistic Association, Inc. shall be an ex-officio member of all committees of Keith Fordham Evangelistic Association, Inc.

Sec. 5. *Joint Undertakings.* Keith Fordham Evangelistic Association, Inc. may, through Board action, participate in joint projects or programs with other groups, corporations, agencies, or organizations. The Board of Directors shall designate Keith Fordham Evangelistic Association, Inc.'s representative to work with other groups, organizations, agencies, or corporations and shall authorize such action as may come within Keith Fordham Evangelistic Association, Inc.'s policy, such action to be subject to ratification by the Board of Directors.

Article IX - Conduct of Business

Sec. 1. *Roberts Rules of Order Revised.* All proceedings and other business meetings of Keith Fordham Evangelistic Association, Inc. shall be governed by and conducted according to <u>Roberts Rules of Order Revised.</u>

Sec. 2. *Quorum.* At the following meetings of Keith Fordham Evangelistic Association, Inc., a quorum shall consist of the following number of individuals in attendance of a meeting:

Description of meeting	Number of Individuals in Attendance
Board of Directors	Simple majority
Committees	Simple majority

Sec. 3. *Vote.* At any meeting of the Board of Directors or a Committee, the majority vote of those present shall be required for any action, except in instances in which the Articles of Incorporation, By-Laws, or laws of the State of Louisiana require otherwise. Each duly constituted member of the body shall have one vote.

Article X - Amendment of By-Laws

Sec. 1. These by-laws may be amended from time to time at any meeting of the Board of Directors by the affirmative vote of two-thirds (2/3) of the entire Board of Directors present or by vote of proxy. Any proposed amendment to the by-laws must be submitted in writing 30 days prior to the next meeting.

Keith Fordham Evangelistic Association, Inc.

By:_____

Keith Fordham, President

ATTEST:

_____

Secretary-Treasurer

EXHIBIT A

BY-LAWS
OF
KEITH FORDHAM EVANGELISTIC ASSOCIATION, INC.
STATEMENT OF FAITH

Subscribed to by Each Member of the Board of Directors and Each Officer of Keith Fordham Evangelistic Association, Inc. Each Year

_____

A. I believe the Bible to be the Mind of Christ, and to be the inspired, the only infallible and the authoritative Word of God.